DIALING FOR DATA

DIALING FOR DATA

A Consumer's How-To Handbook on Computer Communications

David Chandler

Random House
New York

Copyright © 1984 by David Chandler

All rights reserved under International and Pan-American Copyright Conventions.
Published in the United States by Random House, Inc., New York and
simultaneously in Canada by Random House of Canada Limited, Toronto.

*The graphics in this book are from nineteenth-century line drawings
published in the Dover Pictorial Archives Series and reproduced
by permission of Dover Publications, Inc.*

Library of Congress Cataloging in Publication Data

Chandler, David Leon.
Dialing for data.

Includes index.
1. Data transmission systems.   2. Information
networks.   I. Title.
TK5105.C43   1984   384   84-42659
ISBN 0-394-72774-6 (pbk.)

Manufactured in the United States of America

23456789

FIRST EDITION

CONTENTS

5008090

DIALING FOR DATA

CHAPTER 1

What's Out There?

LET ME SAY THIS right away: twenty months ago I could barely use an electric typewriter. My largest experience with high technology was the fold-down sink on an Amtrak train. An "Apple" was something people ate, and I had never heard the term "microcomputer" until I bought one in the summer of 1982. I have been a writer, reporter and correspondent for twenty years, but it had never occurred to me that I could sit at my desk at home or in a hotel room and at the press of a button zap 3,000 words to New York faster than my eyes could blink at the screen.

But that was only the beginning of it. I had even less idea that the computer could gather information for me.

The getting of information is the reporter's special turf. Libraries, musty courthouses and obscure government agencies are reporters' hunting grounds. Finding experts that nobody has ever heard of is their special talent. The ability to track and find data in the basements of bureaucracies is a skill gained from experience and patient teaching. It is a black art passed down from older editor to younger reporter, generation after generation. We've all seen reporters in the movies—like Hildy Johnson in *The Front Page*—prowling the courthouse for news.

But it is no longer that way. Somewhere along the line Hildy nodded off, and while Hildy dozed they raised the shades and the musty courthouses went public. The hard-to-find experts put their names in the Electronic Yellow Pages for all to see. Now any rosy-cheeked rookie with a computer connection can gather more enlightenment while having a cup of coffee than Hildy could in a week of roaming corridors.

THE NEWS CONNECTION

When connected to information services such as The Source, CompuServe or Dow Jones News/Retrieval, your terminal can deliver the news faster than radio, television or the newspapers.

The information is provided by three major wire services: Dow Jones, the Associated Press (AP) and United Press International (UPI).

As you might expect, Dow Jones addresses its reports to the business community and focuses on national and international events.

UPI covers those topics equally well and, in addition, offers separate wires of news and sports from each of the 50 states. The wires of both services can be searched by topic and, in the case of UPI, by state as well.

The most disappointing of the wires is the AP, which is carried on the CompuServe information service. It has only meager search abilities and no state-by-state news. It's mostly a jumble.

An information revolution is occurring in the world. At no time in human history has so much information been available to so many individuals. Not even the boldest futurists will risk their reputations by trying to predict where it will lead. But for now, there are benefits ranging from the simple to the profound, for you and me.

In the fall of 1984 there were more than 1,400 electronic libraries accessible by phone from "terminals" and from "home," "personal" and "small business" computers—systems ranging in cost from $100 to $10,000. The libraries, called "data bases," contain the equivalent of more than 90 million reports ranging in size from single paragraphs to books. The total amount of information is twice that held in the Library of Congress. Furthermore, virtually all of it is updated regularly, often on a daily or weekly basis. Collectively, the data bases constitute the greatest collection of information in the history of the world. And anyone with the desire can join, for a relatively low investment of time and money.

However, be advised that it's not necessarily easy. On a difficult-to-learn scale of one to ten, getting a picture on a television set would rate a one and flying a jetliner a ten.

"COMPUTERS" AND "TERMINALS"

A computer is an electronic or mechanical device used to perform high-speed arithmetic and logical operations. A "computer system" is composed of a computer (or computers) coupled with peripheral equipment, such as disk drives, printers and terminals. A "terminal" is an electronic device used by a person to send or receive information from a computer system. A terminal usually consists of a keyboard connected to a television monitor and/or printer.

On that scale, using the simplest microcomputer system, complete with telecommunications, will rate a three. Operating more complex systems would rate a four (equivalent to learning to drive a car) and higher.

It is only about one notch more difficult to learn "telecommunications," meaning the exchange of information between computers. The hard part is learning how to use computers. The easy part is communications, which in its basics is no more complex than a citizens band radio.

That's what this book does: it explains the basics. It describes the information that is out there, how to find it and how to get it at the cheapest cost. It is a straightforward report to the reader of my own research on computer communications. There will be no pretense at an erudition I

don't have. When I don't know something and haven't been able to find out, I'll say so. And that will happen from time to time.

There will also be moments when you, the reader, will become confused and intimidated while working with an information system. That's part of the game. Everyone has those experiences, and we'll discuss them.

Let's begin by pointing out that computers are not put on earth to save us time. Computers use up our time because there are so many things we can do with them. They are a time sink. They drain time away. I can write a letter three times as fast with a pen or typewriter as with a computer. That's because I make no embellishments. I write it, mail it and go have a beer. On a computer, it doesn't work that way. I experiment with type faces, page spacings, create letterheads, sometimes insert pie charts and bar graphics. I keep fiddling with it until I run out of time. The importance of the letter itself is exceeded by the fun and education of messing with the computer.

Another thing to bear in mind is that computers don't do our thinking. We think for them. What the computer does is process information.

It is a communications machine. And it's changing things as surely as did the telephone. It wasn't that long ago when our ancestors were hooting at each other through the shell of a conch or yodeling across valleys. Now, with computers, we talk to men on the moon.

Twenty years from now, anything before the 1980s is going to be regarded as the Dark Ages. With an inexpensive computer small enough to hold in a lap, we can communicate with electronic libraries containing the equivalent of 50 million books, articles, reports and abstracts. Using that same computer, or any of 150 other brand-name machines, a woman in Georgia can send, via electronic mail, a letter that will reach Oregon in eight seconds, as opposed to a two- to eight-day ride with the U.S. mail.

On a street in downtown San Francisco, a man in a phone booth uses a computer to dial a number that quickly gives him a video-screen listing of all flights to Mexico City and the costs.

Computers in the home or office can talk to one or more other computers across the street, across the country or on the other side of the world. You can sit in your living room and tap a couple of buttons to watch your TV set display the latest news and sports even before they appear on news shows. You can check restaurant menus and hotel listings, do banking, order from department stores, check airline schedules or look at what movies are playing in town and what critics had to say about them. It's literally as easy as turning on the television set.

At an upscale hotel in Chicago, a traveler opens the door to her room.

THE WEATHER CONNECTION

Weather reports and forecasts compiled by the National Weather Service are delivered regularly to terminal users by several on-line information services, including The Source, Dow Jones and CompuServe.

The reports aren't much different from what you get from newspapers, television or radio. But there are three exceptions:

One, you can read reports on any section of the country. If you're in Los Angeles, for example, and flying to Chicago in the month of March, it helps to know if it's snowing or not.

Two, you can call up the reports 24 hours a day, seven days a week.

Three, several services at extra cost offer extensive weather reports for persons with special interests, such as farmers and flyers.

She walks over to a keyboard in front of the television set. She turns on the TV, then touches the keyboard's "on" button and registers the number of a major credit card.

A list of messages—Telex, TWX, mailgrams or other "electronic mail"—appears on the TV screen. Using the terminal, the traveler calls up each message, reads it and then types out replies, sending responses to the home office or to co-workers traveling in other cities. Messages can be sent or received from her home or, for that matter, from any cooperating computer terminal in the world.

The traveler also has at her fingertips an electronic "newspaper" to check Chicago restaurant and entertainment offerings, order flowers or gifts, review stock-market quotations or sports scores and peruse news and sports stories directly from international wire services before they appear on radio or television or in newspapers.

She can perform calculations and trade on the stock and bond markets. And if all else is boring, she can scan the job market, using the computer's electronic classified ads and résumé services.

She could, if she were of such a disposition, dial up a dating service.

This is the present we're talking about, not the future. Computers are rapidly changing the way we live. Contractors are building homes to accommodate them. In Benicia, California, all the $131,000 to $165,000 homes in a 2,450-acre subdivision come with prewired family rooms and bedroom closets to facilitate the installation of computers and peripherals. Dual telephone lines permit people to talk on one line while sending or receiving computer data on another.

Colleges increasingly are requiring computer courses with students expected to buy their own terminals. To make the situation more affordable, discounts (about 30 percent off) are offered by the manufacturers and payments are spread over several semesters. When Apple computer unveiled its innovative Macintosh computer in January 1984, Drexel University immediately announced it was buying 2,000 for its students. Chicago University announced a day later that it was buying a similar number. Apple sold the computers to faculty and students for $1,000 each, 60 percent below the retail price of $2,495.

An optimum use of those computers is to communicate with the electronic libraries or commercial data bases. With few exceptions, the professional bases have been created by companies and agencies that make use of the information themselves. In an effort to generate extra income, they offer it to "outsiders," usually through a vendor such as Dialog or ORBIT.

Those are the data bases that tell us how many volcanoes are erupting on Venus and the number of hairpins manufactured in Formosa in 1938. Or that Formosa is now called Taiwan, and why.

Here is how computer research has been used by some people:

· In a textbook case for homeowners, Richard Bach, author of *Jonathan Livingston Seagull*, and his wife, Leslie, fought the U.S. Bureau of Land Management over a proposed timber cut that would denude parts of a scenic valley in southern Oregon which included their back yard. Using a home computer and two years of their lives, they fought the federals to a standstill, won the fight and ended up with better records on forestry than the lumber companies or the government.

· A woman in West Virginia, Emily Huston, uses her Apple computer daily to monitor 250 stocks. A private investor whose sole occupation is to trade and invest for herself and a few members of her family, she uses her computer to keep track of her portfolio and trading record. At the end of the year, she punches a button, a few pages come out of the printer and she sends them to her tax accountant. The profits she walks to the bank.

· A woman executive in St. Louis had time on her hands and, as sometimes happens, she found herself drifting into frequent daydreams about an old beau. She knew that he was a building contractor but she hadn't seen him in ten years and didn't know where he lived. Turning to her desktop IBM, she punched up a few commands to search the Electronic Yellow Pages, a compilation of all yellow-pages directories in the country, which contains the name, address, telephone number and other data on more than 10 million businesses. It took her less than four minutes to find him. He was in Guam. She never called. It was just a daydream.

· A Florida truck driver, irked by a speeding ticket from a radar-wielding cop, used his computer to prove that police radars across the United States exceed microwave safety limits established by the federal government.

· In the State of Washington, a group called Tilth formed an alternative Grange to offer farmers agricultural information.

· In Chicago, Denver and Atlanta, groups were using data bases to set up job-skills banks, to fight discriminatory lending practices and to get funds for neighborhood rehabilitation projects.

What we've stumbled on here is a democracy of information—a revolution planned by no one but which promises dramatic, if unforeseeable, results. It's as if the inventions of print, radio and television were compressed into a few years and suddenly released to the people all at once.

Throughout history, information has been power, and its use has been jealously guarded by those in control. Depending on whose history we're talking about, we had and have Mysteries of the Priesthood, Official Secrecy Acts, Classified Information, For-Your-Eyes-Only, Industrial Espionage, Swiss Bank Accounts and the Mafia Omertá.

An example is the Pentagon Papers, a report on secret negotiations between the United States and North Vietnam during the Nixon Administration. The "secrets" were known not only to the governments of the United States and Vietnam but to other interested governments as well. The sole interested party that didn't know the secrets was the American public. The Nixon Administration fought all the way to the Supreme Court in its unsuccessful attempt to suppress publication.

Nixon did only what every President before and after him did. And this is in America, a nation that extends freedom of speech, press and information beyond any historical precedent. Try to get a counterpart of the Pentagon Papers published in the Soviet Union.

Government is a frequent controller of information. Today, by law, the dissemination of information in print is controlled to a greater or lesser degree by all governments, with the least control exerted in the United States where the Constitution protects freedom of speech. Television and radio content is likewise controlled by all governments.

Governments, however, are not the only modern controllers of information. Nearly all powerful interests, ranging from organized religions to labor unions to private businesses, protect and restrict the flow of information.

A shift in the historical pattern of guarding information occurred, however, in 1981, when computerized information compiled by industries and agencies in Canada and Europe, but primarily the United States, began to be released to the general public.

Almost unnoticed, information began to slip into the hands of anyone who (1) had access to a small computer; (2) had a device, called a "modem," (for modulator/demodulator of sound signals) that converts the computer's electrical signals into tones that can be carried on the telephone line; (3) knew the phone number of a data bank; and (4) had a password to the data bank's computer. Hooked together, the person and the system practice what is called "telecommunications."

Almost any computer, from a $49 Radio Shack model to the grandest mainframe, can easily be connected to the phone system. All it takes is a set of instructions and a modem.

The growth is rapid. Virtually every computer built today has a modem connection. Within ten years, probably less, virtually every computer will be hooked up to a phone, or be capable of it. More and more computer terminals are being designed with phones built in.

Meanwhile, prices are dropping. In an ancient era, two years ago, my wife Mary and I paid $2,400 for an Apple II system, which included a disk drive, monitor and printer. For those times, it was a very good price. Today we can buy an improved and updated version of the same Apple II system for $900 and the prices continue to fall.

THE SPORTS CONNECTION

Much to my surprise, I've found that the computer information services don't deliver sports scores as fast as television does, particularly cable television.

Sports news is carried in massive quantities on Dow Jones, UPI and the AP, but for some reason they are slow in putting up the line scores.

What they do offer is full-text sports stories which you may never see in the mass media. Indeed, through UPI's 50-state sports wire, you can call up stories on particular athletes, teams or events, including state high school tournaments.

An exception to the above is the Dow Jones Sports Report, operated as a separate part of Dow Jones News/Retrieval. It costs $75 extra to join, but it provides fast scores and the same information carried to newspapers by the UPI sports wire.

Communications, a continuing saga

As prices decline, sales of modems nearly double each year. A study by Dataquest Inc. of California forecast a compound annual growth rate of 70 percent between now and the end of 1986.

The growth of the telecommunications industry is spurred on one side by dropping prices and on the other by a mushroom explosion of information services. New data bases are created almost weekly as a newspaper here, a university there, computerizes its library and makes it available—at first to the few and then to the many.

We will tour all of the major information services, each of which is different in what it offers but typically includes a selection of news, sports, feature stories, shopping transactions, travel services and games.

Those services can offer real returns on the dollar. For example, the user can receive comprehensive reports on any of 3,100 common stocks within minutes at a cost of less than $7 per hour. To duplicate the job manually would cost hundreds of dollars. And shopping via telecommunications for low airline fares has saved me hundreds of dollars.

We'll also look at ways to avoid getting ripped off by shady vendors ranging from multimillion-dollar manufacturers of hardware and software to the neighborhood store. It's a boom industry that rivals the used-car business in its population mix of sharks, sleazes and decent folks with, unfortunately, the latter being a distinct minority.

Indeed, the computer boom has created a new American criminal class. In a further chapter, we'll look at ways to navigate that territory.

CHAPTER 2

Basic Information

THERE IS A GLOSSARY at the back of this book that defines terms ranging from acoustic coupler to zero bit. The list is necessary because this era (the Information Age, as it is being called, but not, by God, by me) is pumping new words into our language faster than any event since the discovery of the Americas.

In that sense, our situation is not much different from that of English ladies and Cavaliers, sitting in the coffee houses 300 years ago, studying Pall Mall and furrowing their brows over words like tomahawk, tobacco, hammock, potato, hickory and wigwam. Different times breed different words. And our times are different.

There are people still alive today, although not a whole lot of them, who were kids when Wyatt Earp and Doc Holliday shot it out with the Clantons at the O.K. Corral. Apache raids and the Alaskan gold rush were events of our grandparents' time. Jupiter flybys and world-wide telecasts of Olympic games are events of ours. The average life style of our grandparents was closer to that of Cro-Magnon man than it is to ours today.

The change has been greater than any that the science-fiction writers were able to predict for the future or imagine on some other planet.

The difference is staggering, but we never think about it. Let's play a game, as I did with my wife. "Mary," I asked, "pretend you could go back a hundred years and visit relatives. What would you take?"

She thought a moment. "Is the idea to show them what the future is like? Or to impress them?"

"Both. But you are limited to twelve items."

"A gasoline-powered electric generator. A television system with home recorder and movies. A video tape of men on the moon and another tape of the atomic bomb. How many is that?" she asked with a pause.

"Five."

"A telephone. An automobile. A map of the United States showing the Interstate System. A supermarket photo. A home computer. An air conditioner and a dishwashing machine."

Her list was virtually unchallengeable. The electric generator was inspired. So was the supermarket photo. Back then, almost every family grew or slaughtered at least a portion of its own food. Today hardly anybody does. I thought a radio would be important, but there would be no broadcast stations for it to receive.

Would you agree with her? Or would you have a different list?

I might quibble with a few of the items. Post–World War II medical advances, from miracle drugs to laser surgery, should be represented somehow. So should the ball-point pen. I'm not too sure about including the telephone and the automobile. Both had been invented by the 1880s and were in limited use.

But the point of the game is that many of the items couldn't be imagined by our grandparents. The trip to the moon, yes. Space travel had been a subject of popular fiction for centuries and the Jules Verne novels of Grandma's day included *From the Earth to the Moon*. The launch pad was near Cape Canaveral, Florida. Really.

But atomic energy, television and modern jet travel? Not a chance that the old folks would have foreseen that. Even further beyond their vision would be the computer, particularly the personal ones which can be owned by any family.

They are new. They need some explanation. And that is what the next few chapters will be about.

At its simplest, a computer is an apparatus that can perform high-speed mathematics and logic. It receives information from an external source and processes it with minimal human participation. It differs from calculating machines, such as abacuses, slide rules and those little hand-held jobs from Korea, in that it can perform more than one function at a time.

JARGON

New events, like the discovery of America or the current computer market, breed new words, often in unexpected ways. The word "Yankee," for instance, is a ricochet that traveled to the New World as the word "English." The North American Indians, however, couldn't pronounce English, so they called the Pilgrims Yengees. The Pilgrims thought Yengees was the Indian word for white people and mentioned it in letters home, spelling it in a variety of ways as was the custom of those nonstandard times. Some of those letters got into the pages of the newspaper Pall Mall as Yankees, meaning North American colonists of English descent. And thank you for listening.

A computer isn't a terminal, although a terminal is what most people think of when they envision a computer. A terminal is the device used to send and receive information to and from a computer. At its simplest, a terminal is a keyboard and a monitor, or a keyboard and a printer. Terminals and computers are sometimes boxed together, like some of the Radio Shack models. But terminals can operate at great distances from computers.

There are smart terminals and dumb terminals. The dumb terminal does little more than receive and send information. The terminals you see at airline counters are dumb.

The smart terminal, depending on how fancy it is, can edit and temporarily store up to several thousand words, produce graphics and perform other chores. Many newspapers, for example, have one or more smart terminals that can display facsimiles of full newspaper pages, including the ads.

The terminals and computers we will be talking about are those that lend themselves to "telecommunications," which is jargon for having two or more computers talk to each other, generally over phone lines. To do that requires more than a computer. It requires a system. The computer itself is only part of a system and many a poor stiff has bought a $200 computer only to learn that a fully operating system can cost $1,000 and more. It is easy, however, to have a fully operating telecommunications system including a printer for $600 or less, and since 1980 the price has dropped at an average of 20 percent per year.

Which system is best? The one that is best for me is one that can do word processing, telecommunications, play a few games and print professional manuscripts.

But I have a friend who rarely does word processing. He runs a sports equipment store and uses a network of Apple computers that operate as cash registers and keep up-to-the-moment records on his inventory and his inventory needs. He uses telecommunications as I do, for information services and electronic mail. But he also uses it to avoid going into his store every day. Working with a small portable computer that he keeps at home, he calls up his daily cash receipts and collects mail and memos from the office staff. Then he leaves his instructions for the next day. His needs are different from mine. Personal computer systems tend to be just that, personal.

Basically, computer systems do the following tasks:

- word processing

- data processing

- business projections

- communications

- education

- recreation

- graphics design

Early Display Device

A system should be designed, first, to meet the needs of the user. Deciding which brand of components to buy (computers, printers, software and the like) depends on the prices and services prevailing locally. And on a particular component's ability to perform specific tasks.

When I say "personal," damn it,
I mean PERSONAL!

An Apple II series, for example, isn't a good choice for word processing but is a superior choice for communications, education and recreation. Xerox PCs, on the other hand, are excellent word-processing machines but inferior in some areas where the Apple IIe is strong—and they are a lot more expensive. The popular IBM PC is quite good at business projections, called "number crunching," but is weak in word processing because of a non-standard keyboard.

The stuff that you can actually touch in a system is called the hardware. The rock-bottom basic hardware needed for a system is:

1. A computer.
2. A terminal, usually a keyboard and monitor but sometimes, especially in portables, a typewriterlike printer.
3. A telephone.
4. A modem, which is the device that literally allows the computer to send and receive sounds via the telephone.

If the computer doesn't have a built-in printer, and few modern ones do, it is advisable to have a separate printer. Otherwise, a lot of handwriting will be needed to record the information received and dispensed.

None of this will do any good, however, unless there is software to run it. Software is the set of coded instructions that tells the computer what to do. Software is synonymous with program. I am writing this book with word-processing software, or a program, which tells the computer that when I touch the letter "A" on the terminal it should record the letter "A" in its temporary memory and display it at a particular place on the terminal screen.

For telecommunications we need a communications program that will at the least send and receive words and numbers.

Additional programs will be needed for specialized uses. I use the computer to send reviews, articles, news reports and book chapters to publishers in other cities. To do that, I need a word-processing program so that I can write the articles in advance and store them in an electronic file. I then use the communications program to send a copy of the file to an editor.

My friend who runs the sporting goods store invests in the stock market. He uses special Dow Jones software, which creates and maintains its own electronic files, to keep tabs on his stock holdings.

In the next few chapters, we'll examine and explain recommended hardware and software. We'll also take "tours" of the information services by showing on the printed page what it looks like to go on-line. Most of these calls, yours and mine, will be made to the local number of a "packet network."

The packet network functions as a switchboard to connect us to an information service or data base. There are three major networks of this type in the United States: Telenet, which is operated by the GTE Corporation, a $20 billion communications company; Tymnet, operated by Tymshare, Inc., a California company with $500 million of annual business; and Uninet, a division of United Telecom Communications in Kansas City, which didn't send me its annual report but appears to be more than solvent.

From our perspective, all three operate the same way. Let's take a look at Telenet. The looking costs nothing.

STEP ONE   I dial a local access number that I have obtained by looking up GTE Telenet in the phone book. I wait for the display screen of my system to inform me that I have established a connection.

WHAT YOU SEE	WHAT I TYPED
TELENET	(*This indicates the connection is made. I then hit the "Return" or "Enter" key on my terminal twice to signal that I am ready to communicate.*)
TERMINAL?	(*Telenet is asking what type of terminal I am using. Such questions from the host system, in this case Telenet, are called "prompts." I enter the term D1, which on the Telenet system is the code for virtually all popular computers. If I were accessing Tymnet I'd enter the letter A. Uninet requires no terminal identifier.*)
	D1
@	(*The "at" sign is Telenet's request for more information. It is asking which computer or information service I want to reach.*)

At that point, were we to continue, we'd enter a code given to us by The Source, CompuServe or whatever. For our purposes, Telenet and the other packet services aren't information services. They can only connect us to information services.

To go further, we need to join one or more information services such as The Source. In return, The Source will give us a code, for example "C 301 38," which will link Telenet and The Source. The Source also will give us a personal password to use once we are connected, or "logged on," to The Source. The procedure varies from data base to data base and will be described in detail in later chapters.

CHAPTER 3

The Hardware

PERSONAL COMPUTERS were first marketed in 1974, when the MITS Corporation of Albuquerque, New Mexico, introduced the Altair computer in the form of a kit, which the buyer put together.

Altair was a small manufacturer of electronics kits for hobbyists, and the new kit's hardware design was poor and unreliable. According to *The Encyclopedia of Computer Science and Engineering,* the documentation verged on the unintelligible and the whole thing seemed like a joke. Even the name Altair was taken from a fictitious planet that appeared in an episode of the TV series *Star Trek.*

But the notion of a computer for the masses was born, an act that put the amazing capabilities of the computer into the hands of the individual at affordable prices.

Just before Christmas of 1974, the Altair was featured as the cover story of *Popular Electronics* magazine, and the little company was overwhelmed with orders.

As the Altair gained attention other companies came out with similar kits. Still more companies introduced software to run on the Altair or offered expansions to the Altair hardware. Computer stores opened all over the nation, particularly in the high-tech enclaves around Boston and San Francisco.

In September 1975 *Byte* magazine appeared, specifically founded to report and discuss personal computing and microcomputers. Hobby clubs sprang up around the nation.

In 1977 Commodore, a major manufacturer of hand-held calculators, announced it would market a complete computer, the Commodore Pet. Almost immediately, the Tandy Corporation, which operates the Radio Shack electronics stores, announced it would market a microcomputer called the TRS-80. In the same year, two California technicians, Steve Jobs and Steve Wozniak, began marketing a small computer that hooked onto the TV. They called it an "Apple."

For the next three years those computers had the market virtually to themselves. Then in 1981, IBM, Xerox, Hewlett-Packard and Victor introduced micros.

All of this action was based on technology that began with the development of the transistor in 1948 at the Bell Laboratories and the Lincoln Laboratory at the Massachusetts Institute of Technology.

The transistor was a tiny amplifier formed on the surface of a semiconductor such as pure germanium or silicon. It was hundreds of times smaller than the vacuum tube which it replaced. In the mid-1950s, aided by photographic-etching technology, engineers developed the first integrated circuit, called an IC or a "chip." Open a computer and inside you'll find mostly electronic circuit boards and "chips." A chip is a small silicon flake upon which a large number of electronic circuits has been etched. The circuits are so tiny that their connection points often can be seen only with a microscope. You won't see them at all because the chip is encased in a hard plastic "sandwich" with metallic connectors running down each side. They are sort of flat, black rectangular things that look like robot beetles with too many legs.

Chips can do two things: store information and process information. Chips that can do both are called processing units.

Chips deal with information in units called "bits" and "bytes." A bit (short for binary digit) is either the numeral zero or the numeral one. The pulsing of electronic circuits between zero and one, or "on" and "off," is how the computer operates.

Zeroes and ones can be translated as numbers or capital and lowercase letters of the alphabet (and other symbols) into a series of ones and zeroes, on and off pulses. For example, the capital letter "Y" is 01011001 and lower case "e" is 01100101. These standardized, 8-bit character codes are called bytes.

The most important of the chips is the CPU, the Central Processing

Unit. It is the core of the computer brain, calling up and processing information and instructions stored in the memory cells of the computer. It works much like our own mind, which reviews and stores our various sensory perceptions and calls up memorized information for action. On certain computers, the CPU can see, hear, sense the touch of a hand or feel temperature changes. With the proper sensors, a computer can comprehend anything that can be measured by numbers, including the loudness and tone of a voice, the pressure of a hand or the degrees of temperature. CPUs currently in common use can process more than one million pieces of information per second.

When the salesman starts talking about "8-bit" and "16-bit" microprocessors, he is talking about the CPU chip and the amount of information it can handle at once. Eight-bit computers dominate the market but are being succeeded rapidly by 16-bit computers. Nevertheless, one is not necessarily better than the other. It's rather the difference in cooking stoves. For some people a simple hot plate is all that is needed. Most of us, however, require a larger stove with four burners and an oven. Some want even more capability, adding restaurant-size ranges, top and bottom ovens and a microwave. But if you don't need the extras, and don't expect to need them for a couple of years, why pay for them?

The distinction between 8-bit and 16-bit and soon-to-arrive 32-bit processors is one that few users ever consider. But it might be useful to know that until recently most large mainframe Fortune 500 computers grabbed information 32 bits at a time. Smaller business minicomputers were happy with 16 bits and personal computers used 8 bits.

In the fall of 1981, however, IBM introduced an 8-bit personal which

CHIPS

The first commercially available microprocessor chip was marketed in 1971 by the Intel Corporation and called the Intel 4004. It was the result of a project to develop chips for inexpensive hand-held calculators.

Microcomputers are often characterized by the number of bits their central processing unit can handle at a single time (technically the width of their data bus). The normal widths for micros are 8 bits and 16 bits with 32 bits due to appear about 1986, notwithstanding Apple Computer's claims of 32 bits for its Lisa and Macintosh computers.

The Intel 4004 was a 4-bit chip capable of handling about 8,000 4-bit operations per second. The Motorola 68000, the chip used in Apple's Lisa and Macintosh, can handle nearly one million 16-bit operations per second.

Since the introduction of Intel's 4004, chips have increased exponentially in complexity while they have decreased exponentially in cost per operation.

used an Intel 8088 chip that performed like a 16-bit. At first, the new chip was regarded as a status symbol with little practical application. But then programmers picked up on it, using the expanded 16-bit technology to present better displays, improved graphics and more functions than were possible with the older 8-bit chips.

IBM started at zero percent of the market, but in less than 18 months, by the end of 1983, it was the leading seller of personal computers in the world and held approximately one fourth of the national and international market.

A great deal of the growth had to do with IBM's marketing expertise and reputation, but none of it would have happened without the improved performance offered by the new chip.

At this point, I am going to give you a series of numbers that are mainly useful in dealing with salespeople.

• 6502 series. These are 8-bit microprocessors used on the Apple II series of computer, the Atari series, and the Commodore Pet and Vic 20. A version, the 6510, runs the Commodore 64.

• Z80 series. Another 8-bit processor which runs many of the Radio Shack models, Heath computers and the Kaypro.

• 8086 and Z8000. These are 16-bit processors that greatly outperform the 8-bits.

• 8088. This is an 8-bit version of the Intel 8086 and powers the IBM PC. Because of innovative design, it performs with the power of a true 16-bit processor and can just plain do a lot more things than the 6502s and the Z8os. But be advised that sales pitches will tell you the IBM PC is a 16-bit machine.

• Motorola 68000. This is the leader of the new wave of processors. According to electronic engineers, it is actually a 16-bit chip that performs like a 32-bit. It is the chip that powers the Apple Macintosh and the Apple Lisa series. Sales personnel like to represent this as a 32-bit processor. Operationally, it's close.

Which is the best for you? If the system is going to work with a lot of data, the 16-bit machines are the way to go. They can keep track of more active memory than 8-bit equipment, are usually much faster and more accurate at "number crunching," which is computerese for working with a lot of arithmetic or mathematical equations. The 16-bit is also more expensive.

If a major use is telecommunications, especially the sending and receiving of words rather than numbers, then the 8-bit is cheaper, usually as good and sometimes better. The money saved can be spent on other home accessories, like a portable bar.

The chip is a processor, and it is measured like a food processor in the kitchen. It can handle so much action at a single time, and no more.

Two other measurements of a computer you will hear about deal not with processing speed but with memory storage, the amount of dough that a food processor can hold in its bowl. The storage units are referred to as ROM and RAM. Both are defined in terms of kilobytes, or how many thousands of characters they can hold at a time. Each character, of course, is a byte.

ROM, meaning read only memory, refers to information permanently

MAGNETS

Computers and their ROM memory can't be hurt by what you do at the keyboard, at least by civilized means. You can, of course, change ROM by obliteration—by bludgeoning it to death with a sledge hammer or erasing it with a magnet. Never, never, never go near a computer system with a magnet unless you want to kill it. All those millions and millions of software instructions can be erased forever by a single sweep of an ordinary magnet.

programmed into the computer on chips. It is software (coded instructions) and can only be read by the computer. ROM is prepared by the manufacturer and cannot be altered on the chip.

RAM means random access memory. It is memory that can be fed or retrieved directly from the computer's electronic storage cells without following a sequence of location protocols. Think of it as going directly to Jail without passing Go while making a circuit of the Monopoly board. RAM is the equivalent of the new information we're working with at any given moment.

For example, you tell the computer to add two plus two. The equation or question punched in on the keyboard becomes part of RAM. It will go away when the computer is turned off. Another means of putting information into RAM is by feeding it a program of information which will instruct the computer how to play a game, draw a picture or provide lists of recipes. Again, when the computer is turned off, the program will go away.

In hardware terms, RAM consists of memory chips that function as rows of electronic mailboxes—the space the computer has to store programs and let us work on those programs.

Random Access Memory

Like ROM, RAM is referred to in groups of 1,000 kilobytes, or 1,000 characters of information—for example, 1,000 letters of the alphabet.

The more RAM, the more extensive the programs that can be run. A typical business program takes between 64K (64,000 characters) and 128K of RAM or more, while games typically require 32K of RAM.

For telecommunications systems, 16K of RAM is adequate, but generally speaking, the more RAM you buy, the better. Virtually all of the new software requires a minimum of 128K of RAM.

A third means of memory storage used by the computer is a filing system. Suppose we need the computer to remember something for future use, such as income tax records. We can't store it in ROM, because that is part of the unchangeable permanent memory and ROM won't accept anything else. RAM will accept it, but the records will vanish as soon as the computer is turned off.

So we turn to a filing system. The earliest home computers, such as the original Apple in 1978, used ordinary tape recorders to record the electronic footprints of our tax records. Tape recorders were annoyingly slow, however, except for games. (The system survives in the form of video game cartridges such as Atari.) The industry turned to bubble memory (see the box on page 27 for an explanation of bubble memory.) By 1981, however, the industry standard had become "floppy disks" and their accompanying "drives."

Floppy disks range in size from three to eight inches in diameter, depending upon the system. They look like the old 45rpm plastic records of the 1950s. They can be purchased blank—to store tax records, for example—or they can be purchased with programs written on them.

Although the tracks are concentric, rather than spiral as on phonograph records, the disks are played much as a phonograph record is played. A unit called a "drive" contains a turntable and a record head which reads magnetic signals on the disk tracks. The drives are sometimes located in the main body of the computer, such as in the IBM PC and the Radio Shack/Tandy series. Other drives, such as in the Apple II series, are separate units connected to the computer by cable.

The computer controls the drive. When a disk is inserted, the drive head is engaged, and at the computer's instruction the drive spins the disk at high speeds to read and write information.

Bubble Memory

BUBBLE MEMORY

Bubble-memory chips are slim films of garnet or similar material magnetized by signals from the keyboard or other input. Bubble memory is capable of storing very large amounts of data in a very small space and is usually found today on portable computers. Bubble memory receives information like RAM, but like ROM, retains it when the power is off.

Like RAM, disks and drives have varying capacities. But even the smallest ones will hold 140K of information, the equivalent of about 50 typewritten pages.

Drives are an important consideration in the purchase of any system. Information recorded on an eight-inch drive normally cannot be read on a smaller drive, and vice versa. Users who switch drive sizes will have a problem in converting information, although much of it can be converted with some ingenuity.

Most of the drives sold prior to January 1981 were eight-inch. Since then, five-and-a-quarter-inch drives have dominated the market. In the past year, however, two large computer manufacturers, Hewlett-Packard and Apple, have introduced units using the three-and-a-half-inch drive as standard.

The new disks, designed by Sony, come in hard plastic shells, which are easier to store, harder to damage and can hold more information than larger disks.

Another feature to consider in buying a computer is how to communicate with the machine. Input devices include ordinary keyboards, joysticks, cordless keyboards which transmit infrared signals, and touch screens. The latter, used on the Hewlett-Packard 150, is relatively new on the PC market but has been in use by airline reservations clerks for years. They touch a passenger's name to get ticket information.

Another input device is the "mouse," an electronic box about two-thirds the size of a pack of cigarettes. It controls an electronic pointer, usually an arrow, on the computer display screen. Pushing the mouse slightly around the desk moves the pointer. When the pointer stops at a command on the screen, such as the command "Save," you push a button on the mouse and the computer permanently stores the information you have given it. The mouse became popular in 1983, when Apple introduced its innovative Lisa computer system. I scorned this particular device until I actually tried one. The Apple versions are the only ones I've tried and they are magnificent for all kinds of work, including word processing.

The innovation of the future, which is already here, consists of having a two-way conversation with the computer, as the astronauts and the computer Hal did in the movie *2001: A Space Odyssey.*

Digital Equipment Corporation (DEC), for example, manufactures a Hal for use with its office computer systems and with IBM and Wang office systems. The $4,000 system, called DECtalk, is programmed to recognize and use most words in an American businessman's vocabulary, including proper names. You talk to it and it talks to you, speaking in eight available voice ranges, including a child's, a woman's and a deep baritone.

Among its uses: executives can call from any touch telephone and ask for electronic mail messages; brokers use it to give quotes to customers; salespeople obtain inventory information; and banks provide customers with balances and other services.

Voice command is more than a gadget, and in the near future it will supplement, but not replace, the primary input method used by computers: the trusty old QWERTY keyboard that has been confronting typists since 1873.

Keyboards range in size from primitive 44-key calculator-like devices to two-foot wide, state-of-the-art consoles that one conducts like an orchestra.

Some keyboards are attached to the computer itself, such as in the

THAT DAMNED QWERTY KEYBOARD

One of the things that have survived since Grandma's day is the non-alphabetical QWERTY keyboard. Used as standard in most nations with a Roman alphabet, it was devised or concocted by Christopher Sholes, a Milwaukee, Wisconsin, newspaper editor. In 1868, Sholes and two colleagues received a patent for the world's first commercially practical typewriter. Its keys, all capitals, were arranged alphabetically in the now familar circular basket. Sholes soon found, however, that the alphabetical arrangement caused the keys to collide. As a solution, he turned to the centuries-old "printer's case," designed so that frequently used letters, such as "a" and "e," are separated by lesser-used letters. Sholes and his colleagues designed the new keyboard and basket accordingly. The improved typewriter was first marketed in 1873. Its keyboard, as you see, is logical after all.

Early Keyboard

Apple II series and on most portable computers. Most desk top computers, however, have detached keyboards.

Keyboards should be selected to one's personal tastes. But generally, detached are more comfortable than attached. And bigger is better. The more keys, the easier the job.

Third-party keyboards, made by someone other than yourself or the computer company, also can be purchased separately for certain popular computers such as the Apple II series and the IBM PC, both of which have shortcomings in their standard keyboard models.

Now that we've discussed the different features of computers, which is the best? At latest count, there were more than 150 different brands of computers on the market. People who write and advise about computer systems are fond of saying that the hardware doesn't matter that much. They say, "Focus on the task and buy the hardware to fit."

Well, that's not entirely correct. All computers perform the basic tasks, as outlined in chapter 2. If word processing is a primary task for you, then any system above the $1,000 price range will do a professional job.

The same is true for other basic tasks, such as data storage, business projection, education or graphics design.

Some computers, such as the Eagle PC or Texas Instruments PC, do better at word processing than, say, the IBM PC, which gives better business programs. For graphics design, I've seen nothing that can equal the Apple Lisa or Macintosh. At the risk of repetition, let me say that the computers are personal. Buying one is not unlike buying a car. They'll all do the same basic job. We all assume that and make our buying decisions based on other factors, such as price, aesthetics, dealer service and general reputation.

CHAPTER 4

Modems and Software

ALL OF THE WORDS of the *Encyclopaedia Britannica* can be transmitted from Washington, D.C., to New York in one second by a light-wave optical fiber telecommunications link now in service. Perhaps equally amazing is the common ability to pick up a telephone and talk to virtually any place in the world, including Antarctica.

The technology of such telecommunications is rooted in the nineteenth century, beginning with the invention of the telegraph by Samuel Morse. Morse's code was the first instance of sending alphabetical letters and numbers by electrical signal. The code was composed of long and short pulses of electricity symbolizing dots and dashes. Most of the letters of the alphabet could be represented by two or three such pulses, a fact that made Morse easy to learn and easy to use. Sort of.

Magazine illustrations of the era envisioned a telegraph in every home and every office. But most people, including clerks and secretaries, didn't want to take the time to learn Morse or to translate it into English. So Morse's telegraph was eventually replaced by something easier to use: the Teletype, which allowed complete printed messages to be transmitted.

It was as easy to use as a typewriter. But because of this very fact, it required more characters than the simple Morse code. There had to be characters to move the paper, return the carriage and announce the start of a character or word.

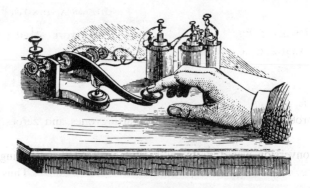

In 1880 the Frenchman J.M.E. Baudot invented a code to do just that. Each character was represented by five binary digits. For example, the letter A was the numeral 1 followed by four zeroes, or a positive pulse followed by four negative pulses. The letter B was zero, zero, one, one, zero. And so on. Baudot was faster than Morse and could transmit over longer distances because it used less power. Furthermore, it could add control characters to drive the teletype.

But there still wasn't a Teletype in every home. It was too expensive. And probably just as important, a lot of people didn't want to learn to type. What they wanted was something like the telephone. They knew how to talk. But Baudot worked on telegraph, not telephone, lines.

And thus it has remained until just about now. There still are no, or few, Teletypes in the home. Very few telegraphs, too. But as early as World War II, Bell Labs, the U. S. Navy and other enterprising go-getters began communicating with computers and found the Baudot Code was no longer sufficient.

When the binary computer was developed, one of the prime applications required was communication between machines. To this end, another code was invented, the American Standard Code for Information Interchange, or ASCII (pronounced Ask-Kee).

Because binary computers are off-on devices, they deal in powers of the number two, one for on, zero for off. The ASCII code represents numbers in eight binary digits, eight being the number two to the third power.

Thus, in ASCII, the letter A becomes 01000001.

The expansion to eight bits of ones and zeroes (a byte) allowed ASCII to convey much more information than simply the letters of the alphabet and numbers. Various instructions, such as "Turn on the printer" and "Cancel what I just said," could be transmitted computer to computer.

ASCII worked fine for computers but didn't work at all on phones. To communicate, computers were "hard-wired," connected together by a cable. Telephones, although they sat in virtually every business and home in America, couldn't transmit ones and zeroes, or ons and offs. Telephones transmit sound, not the absence of it.

The problem was overcome by converting ones and zeroes to sound pulses.

The conversion was done by a "modulator." At the receiving end, the sound was converted back to ASCII by a "demodulator." Thus the term "modem," for modulator/demodulator.

A modem may be a printed circuit-board that fits inside the computer. Or it may be a separate device, usually about the size of a paperback book, that connects to the telephone line in one of two ways. A direct-connect modem plugs into a phone jack like an ordinary telephone. An acoustic coupler or acoustic modem taps into the phone line by means of a cradle into which the telephone handset is placed. Whatever it looks like, it connects the computer to the phone line.

When we use ordinary telephone lines we are somewhat restricted as

MODEMS

This is a story with a happy ending where the little guy wins and the bullying phone company gets it in the eye.

Modems were invented by the Bell telephone company, which used them for internal use and regarded them as part of the telephone monopoly. The claim wasn't disputed until the late 1960s after the "acoustic coupler" was introduced by the Carterphone Company, a manufacturer of two-way mobile radios. The acoustic coupler wasn't wired into the phone line but instead sent and received information through the handset of a regular telephone.

Carterphone maintained it wasn't interfering with the Bell patents or monopoly but instead it was merely using existing phone lines in order for its machines, rather than people, to talk with one another.

Bell claimed use of the coupler was illegal and warned that use of one could result in termination of phone service. An old ploy, right?

Well, it sort of worked. Carterphone's customers were indeed scared off and the company went out of business. But then Carterphone did something wonderful. It sued the phone company. The U.S. Supreme Court ruled in favor of Carterphone and said such couplers were legal. More decisions followed and the end result was that modems and a lot of other things that hook into phone lines (like answering machines) became generally available almost simultaneously with microcomputers.

to the speed of data transmission. Until recently, the almost universal transmission rate was 300 bits (about 30 characters) per second. The unit used to measure such transmission speed is called a "Baud" in honor of Baudot.

For most commercial data bases, 300 Baud is still the most common transmission speed. That is rather a slow rate, which moves across the monitor screen just about as fast as a person can read. However, by increasing the Baud rate, we can reduce the time spent on the phone line, and thus reduce costs.

At the current time, you can buy modems which operate at speeds up to 19,200 Baud. Such speed rates, however, are used mostly by mainframes talking with one another. For bulletin board and information service use, 1,200 Baud is about as fast as we can go. The savings, if any, have to be calculated because many of the commercial data bases charge extra for the higher speed.

A 300-Baud transmission sends the equivalent of 30 letters or numbers per second. A 1,200-Baud transmission sends the equivalent of 120 characters per second.

Direct
Connect Modem

It's mainly a matter of cost, and as a practical matter most personal-computer users will do better at 300 Baud until, and when, 1,200 Baud becomes an industry standard.

The telephone modem may not be with us forever. It is also possible for a computer to transmit and receive data over television circuits or radio circuits, or even by a modulated signal over the 115-volt electric power lines that run the computer.

With the split-up of the Bell System there may be a shift to television cable and satellite channels for data communications. But for most users that shift will be many years away. In the foreseeable future, modems are the way to go.

All other conditions being equal, the direct-connect modem works much better than the acoustic modem. However, many hotels and motels have their room phones hand-wired into the wall and there is no phone jack for a direct computer connection. Travelers carrying portable computers, therefore, should be prepared to use the acoustic modems.

It's not a big problem. Desktop computers stay at home or at the office where direct connection is possible. Most portables come with direct-connect modems but offer acoustic couplers as an add-on, usually at the cost of $50 or less.

Most modems connect to the computer by means of an RS-232-C serial interface, built into most computers. The Apple II series is one of the few exceptions. An interface card, costing about $100, has to be added to the Apple in some instances. (The most popular Apple II modems, the Hayes Micromodem II and the Novation Apple-Cat II both come equipped with serial boards, so there is no extra expense.)

Modems, like terminals, come "dumb" and "intelligent." A dumb modem meets the basic requirements of originating a call or answering the phone, and allows switching between half and full duplex. Half duplex refers to one-way transmissions, like a citizens band radio where people must alternate talking and listening. Full duplex is two-way transmission which allows simultaneous conversation, like a telephone.

A selection of duplexes is also available on intelligent modems. An intelligent modem might dial, answer or hang up the phone on command, automatically re-dial the last number or remember an entire phone book of numbers that you select from by name or other code.

Properly programmed, the computer with intelligent modem can dial late at night, when the rates are lowest, and obtain *Wall Street Journal* headlines through the Dow Jones information service, call up your electronic mail, check The Source and other community bulletin boards for

MORE JARGON

Like RAM and ROM, "duplex" is another term of well-known definition but puzzling origin. What it refers to is the flow of information between computers.

Full duplex and half duplex refer to whether or not a modem is sending and receiving at the same time. Half duplex is a one-way-only communication. Think of it as a CB or ham radio where you listen to the other person talk and then press a button so you can talk. Full duplex is two-way communication, like a telephone where either party can speak at the same time.

For our purposes, the main effect of duplex is what you see on the screen. If the duplexes aren't matched up, you won't see what you are sending. You may see nothing, or you may see double images. Full duplex is preferred and is used by virtually all information services. Don't buy a modem unless it offers full duplex communication.

messages, and have it all ready for you to peruse with the morning coffee.

In the answer mode, the intelligent modem can be programmed to answer the phone and receive text files or programs from another computer (which in turn may have been programmed to make the call late at night unattended). Using a modem capable of answering the phone, you can run a bulletin board, a dating service, an employment service or whatever you like without having to be there.

With such a setup, it is possible to use a portable computer or office computer and phone home to receive or leave messages.

When buying a computer, do not assume that everything you need to hook up a modem will be provided. Modems themselves can be used with virtually any terminal or computer. Interfaces, however, are "machine specific," meaning they are designed for specific terminals or computers. You'll also need a cable running from the interface to the modem. Before you buy, make sure all four components are compatible—the modem, the cable, the interface and the terminal/computer.

Some modems are "originate only" devices. They can place a call but can't receive one. Other modems, called "originate/answer," can do both. Most of the time you will originate the call, but the prices between the two types are about the same, so buy "originate/answer." That way, you will be prepared for the few, but usually useful, occasions when you want your system to stand by for a call.

Two other features to look for are "auto-answer" and "auto-dial." Auto-

Acoustic
Coupler

dial is the more common. It allows you to place a call from your terminal. Auto-answer will answer the phone when it rings and automatically connect it to the computer. It is a handy option if you want to query your system from another terminal, or if you want others to do the same. Auto-answers usually can be set to allow the phone to ring a certain number of times before it connects the call to the computer. Such a program allows a person to answer the phone first, but if no one answers, then the computer will.

Of course, the computer will sit there like a dummy until it hears a Baud signal coming from the other end. What the caller will hear is a banshee-like shriek. Most computer communications systems reply only to other computers, and not to voice calls.

When shopping for a modem, I'd recommend the following minimum system:

· Direct connect to the phone line.

· Full duplex capability.

· 300-Baud minimum speed—1,200 is preferable if you can afford it. If you buy a 1,200-Baud modem, be certain that it is 212A-compatible," which means that it can communicate at either 300 Baud or 1,200 Baud and at either half or full duplex.

· FCC approved.

· Auto-dial and auto-answer.

Here is a list of the more popular modems. All are direct connect. I'm listing phone numbers in case you want to call for brochures or other information, but my usual warning prevails: phone numbers may, and probably will, change.

COSYSTEM   An expensive 300- 1,200-Baud system designed for IBM Personal Computer, sold at a list price of $1,845 by Cygnet Technologies of Sunnyvale, Ca., 408-734-9946.

HAYES MICROMODEM II SERIES   Designed for the Apple II series and the best modem for that series. The 300-Baud Micromodem comes with its own software communications program at a list price of $409, but is frequently discounted to about $270. Hayes Microcomputer Products, Norcross, Ga., 404-449-8791.

HAYES SMARTMODEM 300   Designed for any RS-232 serial port, this 300-Baud modem lists for $289 and is frequently discounted.

HAYES SMARTMODEM 1200   An updated version of the 300, which runs at 300 and 1,200 Baud. List price is $699 but it is frequently discounted.

MICROCONNECTION   This comes in several versions, working with the Atari home computer series and the RD 232 ports. It comes with a limited communications program at a list price of $159. Microperipheral Corporation, Redmond, Wa., 206-881-7544.

MODEM II   A Radio Shack modem which provides auto-answer and auto-dial features for TRS-80 computers. It lists at $249 from Radio Shack, Fort Worth, Tx., 817-390-3700.

NOVATION CAT   Designed for RS-232 ports, a popular 300-Baud system listing for $189. Novation also has a 1,200-Baud modem which usually sells for less than $500. Novation, Tarzana, Ca., 818-996-5060.

PERSONAL COMPUTER FILE TRANSFER   An almost universally applicable system for Apples, IBMs, Radio Shacks and other brands, delivering

Baud rates from 110 to 9,600. It comes with its own communications software and sells via mail order for $94.95 from Personal Computer Products of Santa Clara, Ca., 408-988-0104.

PRENTICE P212 An RS-232 modem operating at 1,200 Baud and selling at $595 list from Prentice Corporation, Sunnyvale, Ca., 408-734-9810.

You can use modems without a telecommunications program, but it is like trying to walk with water skis—difficult for some and impossible for the rest of us.

The modems need software, and software needs modems. It is best to shop for both at the same time because one can limit the other. If you select one of the more popular modems, such as the Hayes Smartmodem, software shouldn't be a problem because the Smartmodem is so widely used that most telecommunications programs support all of its functions.

The main thing you want from the software is the ability to support the modem of your choice, the ability to save information on disk for later editing and printing, and the ability to print while receiving information on your monitor.

When shopping for software, try to find out how easy to use the software is and how well organized and indexed the documentation is.

It is also preferable to buy software that will automatically log you onto a data base through the use of "macroinstructions," or, as they are commonly called, "macros." The term refers to condensing a series of instructions into a single command. For example, by touching four keys in succession, a macro will dial a Telenet number, give the proper code to connect to The Source, give The Source a user identification number and password, log onto The Source, check an electronic mailbox for mail and then wait for further commands.

As will be discussed in a later chapter, each data base will have a different sequence of commands and passwords to go through before the user is "signed on" and able to call up information.

The average user will be regularly logging onto a general-purpose data base such as The Source, an electronic mail service such as Telemail, a financial news service such as Dow Jones and a letter-writing service such as MCI Mail. That's a minimum of four data bases, each of which might normally be checked several times a week because each may have personal messages. All this research requires remembering four separate sequences of telephone numbers, data-base code numbers, passwords, a user identification number and a sign-on name.

A far better procedure is to have a communications program, such as the ASCII Professional, that allows you to write the log-on sequence once and then the program, not you, remembers it thereafter.

I use ASCII Pro and have installed the passwords and protocols of 24 different services and bulletin boards in its macro library. I can call any of those by touching four keys in sequence. If it weren't for the macros, I would have to look up the passwords and procedures for each call because I have a memory like a sieve. And I'm also lazy, so I think I wouldn't be getting nearly as much out of the system as I do now.

Here are the most popular communications programs, listed in alphabetical order by manufacturer. If you shop, it's almost always possible to purchase the programs far below list cost.

HELLO CENTRAL For Apple II series and compatibles such as the Franklin. It lists for $99.50 from Howard W. Sam Co., Indianapolis, Ind., 800-348-8558.

APPLE-IBM CONNECTION For Apple IIs, IBMs and compatibles. It lists at $250 from Alpha-Software, Burlington, Ma., 617-229-2924.

ACCESS III For the Apple III computer, listing for $150 from Apple Computer Company, Cupertino, Ca., 408-996-1010.

CONTEXT MBA Part of an integrated program for IBMs and Hewlett-Packards, with all the MBA software listing for $695 from Context Management Systems, Torrance, Ca., 213-378-8277.

ASCOM Suitable for virtually all personal computers, listing for $175 from Lifeboat Associates, New York City, 212-860-0300.

MICRO/COURIER For Apples, IBMs and Radio Shacks. This is one of those programs that can send and receive while you sleep and while rates are cheap. Messages can be sent to as many as 100 other computers, provided they, too, have Micro/Courier software. It keeps a record of all messages sent and messages that are ready to be sent. Listing for $250 from Microcom, Norwood, Ma., 617-762-9310.

MICROTERM For Radio Shacks, IBMs and Zeniths, listing for $80 from Micro-Systems Software, Hollywood, Fl., 305-983-3390.

DATA CAPTURE Has programs for the IBM Personal Computer and the Apple II series. The IBM software lists for $120 and the Apple for $65, from Southeastern Software, New Orleans, La., 504-246-8438.

ASCII EXPRESS ASCII won't make calls while you sleep, but it is one of the fastest, most versatile and powerful communications programs on the market. Part of a series of programs including The Professional, listing at $129 from Southwestern Data Systems, Santee, Ca., 714-562-3670.

TRANSEND Has a series of programs for the Apple and the IBM ranging in price from $89 list to $275, from SSM Microcomputer Products, San Jose, Ca., 408-946-7400.

As a practical matter, modems of 300 Baud range in price from $50 to $300. Higher-speed modems are in the $500 range. Communications software can cost from zero dollars (free programs can be found on bulletin boards) to $300 and up. A connecting cable, sometimes required, costs about $35. Thus, with an IBM PC you can begin communicating for approximately $500. On an Apple Macintosh the cost would be about $325.

```
I should have skipped
    this chapter and
had a beer'n'sandwich
     in the park.
```

CHAPTER 5

Computer Choices

THE CORE of the telecommunications systems is the computer. This chapter will list the ones that have come to my attention either through personal tryout or through a favorable review by a consensus of the industry.

It is by no means a complete list. At this writing there are more than 500 models of microcomputers on the market, manufactured by 180 different companies. That's far too many to deal with here.

In choosing a system, you should consider which operating system or systems it uses. As the name indicates, an "operating system" is the instruction program, usually built in as ROM, which controls the overall operation of a computer system.

For example, calculators—although not true computers—have an operating system carrying the instruction for performing various mathematical operations.

If computers were simple, like television sets, we wouldn't need to bother ourselves about operating systems and software. We'd just go out and find the one with the best picture and sound, buy it, bring it home and turn it on.

But it's not that easy. Computers won't give us a picture or any other performance unless we have an operating system to serve as a liaison

IS THERE A FREUDIAN
IN THE HOUSE?

Operating-system software is often called "firmware," if you can believe it. I don't know why. By definition, it distinguishes ROM software from RAM software. But that is already done by the adjectives ROM and RAM. Who makes up these names? RAM? ROM? Software? Firmware? Hardware? There's something to think about here.

between the hardware and the RAM software. The operating system is usually, but not always, built into ROM.

This wouldn't be important to you except that "applications software" is written for a specific operating system. Applications software is used for general tasks, such as word processing, telecommunications, statistical projections and so on. A word-processing applications program written for the Apple II series most certainly won't work on the IBM-PC.

Which system has the most software? A survey published in 1984 by Sofsearch International showed Apple with the largest overall base, having 2,430 programs for home or office applications; 915 for entertainment and 2,161 for education. CP/M offered 3,493 business applications. TRS had 5,047 divided equally among business, education and home/office use. MS-DOS had 3,167, of which 75 percent was business-oriented.

Bearing all that in mind, here is a list of the better computers you'll find on the market. The prices are approximate, and you can probably find discounts on all the machines.

APPLE II SERIES   This is the machine that created the market. It started out as the "Apple," then was succeeded by the II followed by the II Plus, Apple IIe, and the portable Apple IIc. Collectively, the series represents the most popular computer in history. Although the IIs and II pluses have been phased out of production, used models are still found at low prices. For schools and other institutions, they may be bargains. For practical use, I'd stay clear of them. Adding on the necessary updates such as modems and 80-column displays will cost more than a modern computer.

On the other hand, the IIe and IIc are highly recommended among systems in the $1,000 range. They are good buys both intrinsically and technically because more software has been written for the Apple and more people own them than any other computer. As a consequence, it is easier to find help for the Apple than for any other computer. Such

MORE THAN YOU PROBABLY WANT TO KNOW ABOUT . . .

There are almost as many operating systems as there are computers, and their importance is that they determine what kind of software you will be able to use, or "run" in computer jargon, on your system. The most commonly used operating systems are:

• CP/M, an acronym for Control Program for Microcomputers, was invented in 1973 and is the oldest on the market. The CP/M series, which includes CP/M-86 and Concurrent CP/M, runs on more brands of micro than any other system. It is primarily business-oriented.
• Apple DOS, for Disk Operating System, runs on the Apple II series of computers and has more software written for it than any other system.
• TRSDOS, stands for Tandy Radio Shack Disk Operating System. It is used on the TRS-80 series of computers.
• MS-DOS, for Microsoft DOS, with Microsoft being the software manufacturer that designed the program. A version of MS-DOS called PC-DOS runs on the popular IBM PC.

Missing from the above list is the ultra-advanced system for the Apple MacIntosh and Lisa. Technically, however, the Mac and Lisa ROM programs are more than just operating systems and can't be realistically compared with the others.

support and the ease of getting it should be a primary factor in buying a computer.

All IIs have an 8-bit "6502" microprocessor and generate a display 25 lines long by 40 columns wide on the monitor screen. RAM is expandable. Included in the usual discounted IIe system of $1,000 or less are one or more 148K disk drives, 64K to 128K of RAM, a monitor and a "card" inserted inside the computer which allows the computer to generate displays of 25 lines by 80 columns and wider. By Apple Computer Inc., Cupertino, California.

APPLE LISA   A new generation of micro with extraordinary beauty and power while at the same time extremely easy to use. You can't even measure Lisa by the standards of other PCs. It arrives with 512K of RAM, expandable to one megabyte. Its single three-and-a-half-inch Sony drive holds 400K of memory and is expandable with a 10-megabyte internal hard disk. It runs superb software designed for the LISA, the Macintosh and, with adaptation, some of the IBM library. Prices start at $3,500, and for a fully equipped system with modem, printer and a full megabyte of RAM you'll pay about $8,000. That's a lot. But an IBM PC or IBM PC XT somewhat comparably equipped would cost more, although the IBM can't duplicate Lisa totally. Lisa puts you at the forefront of micro technology.

APPLE MACINTOSH   Another beautiful machine. This 18-pound, transportable champion arrives with 128K of RAM expandable to 512K. It is almost as easy to use as a television set and has some of the best software on the market. It is comparable to the Lisa but less expensive and without as much power. It sells regularly for $2,000 and less.

APPLE III   This is an odd computer with amazing strengths and amazing weaknesses. Kind of like an elephant with tiny feet. An 8-bit computer that performs somewhat like a 16-bit, it comes standard with 256K of RAM, dual 148K disk drives, a 12-inch monochrome monitor and a printer port. That system has a list price of $2,695, but I have regularly seen them discounted to less than $1,700. Its keyboard, although attached, is superior in design. The machine is very fast and has a built-in self-testing unit that tells you if anything is wrong the minute you power up. It generates beautiful color graphics. Programmers regard the III with near reverence.

For ordinary users, however, it has meager storage capacity unless you want to add a hard disk costing $1,500 or more. The software is as peculiar as everything else about the machine. Few programs have been written specifically for the III. But it has an emulation mode which allows it to run the vast 5,000-program library of the II Plus. And for about $500 you can add a CP/M card that allows the III to run more than 3,000 business-application programs.

If the price is right, the III can prove to be an interesting hobby with solid business and telecommunications abilities.

COLUMBIA VP   A transportable rated as among the most compatible to IBM PC software and hardware add-ons. With a bundle of quality software, it is selling at discount houses at about $2,700.

COMMODORE 64   A good, inexpensive PC with color graphics and sound capabilities that make it fun to own as a first computer. A system including a disk drive, printer and a modem can be put together for about $650 at discounted prices. The 8-bit Commodore has 64K of RAM, a 25-line-by-40-column color display and an attached 66-key typewriter-style keyboard. Its software, unfortunately, is limited almost entirely to that produced by the manufacturer, Commodore Business Machines of Westchester, Pennsylvania.

COMPAQ   A sturdy 16-bit transportable portable that is one of the most successful duplicators of the IBM PC. It not only runs software designed for the IBM but accepts hardware add-ons built for the PC. The 8-bit/16-bit Compaq comes standard with 128K of RAM, expandable to 640K; two 640K-byte floppy disks; a 9-inch monochrome screen built into the computer; a display of 25 lines by 80 columns; built-in interfaces for high-resolution color monitors, printers and television sets. Its main drawback is a keyboard designed after the awkward IBM keyboard. The two-drive model lists for $3,590. A one-disk is available and lists for $2,495. It is manufactured by Compaq Computer Corporation of Houston, Texas.

EAGLE   A lot for the money. Eagle puts out several PCs, including the Eagle PC, an IBM-compatible with 16-bit processor, 256K of RAM, dual drives, monitor and software and discounted to $2,000. Eagle also offers hard-disk PCs and a transportable, all of which have received raves from reviewers. It has the sharpest monochrome display on the market, except for the Lisa and Macintosh. For people who want an IBM but don't want to spend that much money, Eagle is definitely worth looking at. Its one weakness is inferior manuals, but telephone support is good. By Eagle Computer, Los Gatos, California.

EPISODE   This little-known computer is a favorite of INFOWORLD, the microcomputer industry's top newsmagazine. It is a relatively low-cost PC for small-business and professional use. It comes standard with

IBM "COMPATIBILITY"

In shopping for computers, you'll find that many makers claim their machines are compatible with the IBM personal computers, the IBM PC and IBM PC XT.

In fact, there are different degrees of compatibility, but most computer buyers have one idea in mind when they shop for an IBM compatible: they want a lower-priced machine that can run most, if not all, of the IBM machines' software without modification.

The top three sellers of machines considered closely compatible with the IBM personal computer are Compaq Computer Corp., Columbia Data Products Inc. and Eagle Computer Inc.

Often compatibility gets confused with a machine's ability to run Microsoft Corp.'s MS-DOS, an operating system, or with the background program that controls the basic functions of a computer.

To be compatible, a machine must run MS-DOS, but MS-DOS alone doesn't ensure compatibility. A hundred companies have licensed the right to use MS-DOS on their machines. But before it can run on any but the most compatible computers, IBM software has to be modified by its developers. That can take months, especially in the case of the more sophisticated programs which often sidestep MS-DOS and make direct calls on a machine's hardware. It took Lotus Development Corp. about six months to alter its IBM version of Lotus 1-2-3 for use on another MS-DOS machine.

Computer makers and dealers use Lotus 1-2-3 and Flight Simulator, an education program made by Microsoft, as tests of compatibility.

You can do the same. If you are buying a computer on the basis of IBM compatibility, ask the salesperson to run a copy of the IBM PC version of Lotus 1-2-3 or Flight Simulator. Both programs are popular and the store should have them in stock. If they don't, go to another store or ask that store to get it. That way, you don't have to rely entirely on the salesperson's word on compatibility.

an incredible 1.6 megabytes—that's 1600K—of disk storage. It is an 8-bit, CP/M-based micro with 64K of RAM; dual 5¼-inch drives; onboard calendar clock; built-in interfaces (called ports) for both modem and printer; and a built-in telecommunications program. All that comes at a list price of $2,280 from Epic Computer Products of Fountain Valley, California. It comes without a terminal but will work with a variety of third-party terminals priced from $500.

EPSON QX-10 A marvelous idea that fell on its face and once again proved that Japanese technology may be more hype than reality. Introduced in 1983, the Epson was supposed to set a new standard for PCs.

It came with stunning monochrome graphics, 256K RAM of main memory, dual half-height drives of 380K storage each, built-in clock calendar, built-in printer and modem ports, two operating systems and the highly touted VALDOCS integrated software. In addition, its keyboard looked like the cockpit of the Columbia space shuttle. It was the finest-looking PC this side of the Lisa or Macintosh. All this for a list price of $2,495 and frequently discounted for several hundred dollars less.

But it didn't fly. Primarily designed for word processing, it was slow and often "crashed" (became inoperable), destroying pages and pages of already entered text. Instruction documents were virtually unusable. The combination of sluggishness, destruct tendencies and abysmally bad documentation made several reviewers issue warnings against the QX-10, as if it were hazardous waste.

We include it in this list in the hope that its defects will be cured. It has a lot of promise. But test it thoroughly before you put down one nickel of deposit.

FRANKLIN ACE   The Franklin Company of Pennsauken, New Jersey, puts out two computers, the Ace 1000 and the Ace 1200. Both are Apple II compatible, and the latter also works in a limited way with CP/M systems. Franklins are frequently discounted, and a full system with 64K of RAM and one drive, monitor, software, interfaces and modem should cost less than $1,200. Documentation and manufacturer's support on the Franklin are poor.

HEWLETT-PACKARD 150   This is the "Touch Me!" computer which uses MS-DOS and the Intel 8088 central processor, making it slightly compatible with IBM software. But Hewlett-Packard is an industry giant and has plenty of excellent software in its own right. The system is easy to use and well engineered. It comes with 256K of expandable RAM, two 3½-inch drives, a 9-inch touch screen and is modem-ready. Personally, I don't like the touch screen, and I think the monitor is too small and the price, at $3,995 list, too high.

IBM PC JR   The "Peanut" went to market in 1984 as a competitor to the Apple IIe. It is included here because it is a hot product and some reviewers liked it. More didn't, however. I find it is overpriced and has a surprisingly small memory for a new computer. It has only limited compatibility with the higher-priced IBM PC and PC XT.

The Peanut board has one popular feature: it communicates with the computer via infrared signals. The Peanut has a 40-column display like the old Apple IIs. And like the old Apples, it is designed to hook up to the family television rather than to a monitor. Using the infrared keyboard, the Peanut can be run from the living-room sofa, like a television remote control. IBM has been laboring mightily to overcome some of the difficulties. And third-party groups, such as Keytronics Corporation of Spokane, Washington, are producing larger, full-function keyboards for the Peanut. But why bother? The Peanut, at $1,200 or more per system, is a lemon.

IBM PC AND PC XT The IBM PC is the machine that changed the micro world. It has amazing capabilities, including color business graphics, that make the composition of reports and inventories a joy. It also has a long list of irritating shortcomings, including a notorious keyboard, which doesn't seem to have been designed for touch typists. In sum, the IBM PC is a machine that in its nearly infinite variety of configurations has managed to be all things to all people. There seem few neutrals in the IBM discussion. It's love it or hate it.

It has been denounced as an overpriced, middle-performance computer. But most (approximately 70 percent) of all new software being written is aimed directly at the IBM PCs. Possession of an IBM or an IBM compatible puts you at the head of the high-tech parade. But it will cost you.

The PC is both an 8-bit and a 16-bit machine with a typical system of 256K of RAM, one 180K drive, green 12-inch monitor, color graphics capability and a communications access port, and it costs $2,000. Figure another $1,000 to add a color monitor and a modem.

Its newer and bigger brother, the XT, runs faster, has even greater expansion abilities and comes with more than 10 megabytes of storage. An XT system similar to the above PC configuration would cost $5,000, including color and modem. IBM ships the PC and XT from its Boca Raton, Florida, plant.

KAYPRO SERIES If you're picking a portable based on popularity, Kaypro wins hands down. A favorite with writers, it is ready to work within minutes after unpacking and plugging it in. Entire systems including software and modems have been selling for $1,400 and less. That price will include 64K of RAM, dual drives of 190K storage each, a built-in 9-inch monochrome monitor, built-in printer port and a built-in modem port. That's a lot for the money.

There is no color, but the keyboard is well designed and detachable and the Kaypro runs the well-supported Xerox 820 software. It's a plain-Jane sort of computer with few games or other frills. Its appearance is so Spartan that it looks like a World War II army field radio. Although it has a handle and folds up into a case, it weighs 26 pounds and that hardly makes it portable. "Transportable" is the word currently used.

It is cheap, hardy and reliable. The Volkswagen Beetle of computers. Some like 'em. Some don't. Dollar for dollar, it is hard to beat. The manufacturer is Kaypro Corporation of Solana Beach, California.

MORROW MICRO DECISION   The Morrow offers excellent performance for the money. Its 8-bit, CP/M-based computer can run a wealth of business software, and its list price ranges from $995 to $2,290, depending upon the different configurations of drives and terminals selected. The basic system includes the 64K computer, single disk drive, and a full package of top-quality word processing and business software, and lists for $995. You will need a terminal and a modem for a total basic-system cost of $1,690. A more powerful system, which includes the above plus a second disk drive and 768K of storage, lists at $2,290. It may be the least expensive full-ability system on the market. It is produced by Morrow Designs of San Leandro, California.

NEC APC   This is a dynamite computer, powerful, slick, which is being marketed at aggressively low prices, often below $2,500, and includes a bundle of quality business software. The 16-bit APC model comes with MS-DOS, a single drive and a monochrome monitor at that price. NEC Information Systems, Atlanta, Georgia.

NORTH STAR ADVANTAGE   This is an outstanding business-oriented PC with a 16-bit Intel 8088 processor capable of running thousands of programs, including much of the IBM library. It also has two 8-bit processors in a configuration called the Advantage 8/16. At a list price of $3,400, the 8/16 comes with 128K of RAM expandable to 256K, a superior 87-key keyboard, a 12-inch monochrome monitor and dual disk drives with 720K of storage. Its main drawback is that it can't produce color graphics. The Advantage is produced by North Star Computers of San Leandro, California.

OTRONA ATTACHE   At 18 pounds, the Attache Portable is barely portable but offers impressive memory capacity and fast operations. It is a 64K RAM, 8-bit machine with dual 5¼-inch drives holding 720K of storage. Built-ins include a small 5½-inch green monitor, a clock calendar, modem port and a printer port. There is no color. It is designed like the Kaypro with a detached keyboard folding up against the rest of the PC to form a carrying case. It is a quality product but expensive at $2,995 list. At that price, it should at least include a direct connect modem. But for now, the modem costs extra. The Attache is manufactured by Otrona of Boulder, Colorado.

RADIO SHACK/TANDY   A long line of computers is marketed by Tandy Corporation through its 8,700 Radio Shack stores worldwide. Systems, including computers, modems and software, range in price from the $230 Micro Color 10 to the $3,150 Tandy 2000. The latter is a 16-bit MS-DOS computer with detached keyboard, 128K of RAM and dual drives with a total of 1.4 megabytes of storage. Radio Shack claims the Tandy 2000 runs most software designed for the IBM PC and a comparable IBM system would cost $900 more. In dealing with other Radio Shack computers, however, be warned that buying one is like marrying the corporation. Your software and peripherals, such as printers, all come from Radio Shack and only Radio Shack. But there are some pluses. The Radio Shack sales people, in general, are much more helpful and polite than the industry as a whole. There is usually one Radio Shack outlet in even the smallest cities. And they put out a complete line of machines and software that is competitive in cost and performance and well supported by a single company.

RCA APT   This is not a computer but an "all purpose terminal," which is what "APT" stands for. I include it because it is designed exclusively for telecommunications and comes ready to plug in and run like a TV. A single press of a key can dial a stored number and log on to an information service or another computer. The terminal comes complete with a keyboard, direct-connect modem, auto-dial, auto-answer and originate/answer. That package, which hooks up to a television set, lists at $399 and is regularly discounted. If you want a better display, one 80 characters wide, you can add any standard monitor for discounted costs ranging from $75 up. The problem with this type of terminal is that it has no memory in which to store information received. You can, however, hook up a printer. VCA MicroComputer Products, Lancaster, Pennsylvania.

SCANSET   Like the RCA, this is also an information terminal and not a full-fledged computer. It, too, is designed for people who want nothing more complicated than plugging in a TV set. Scanset arrives as a single package which hooks up to the phone and is operating within minutes. At a list price of $649, the French-manufactured Scanset includes a built-in 300-Baud modem, automatic dialing and log-on to data bases, a built-in monochrome monitor and an attached Chiclet-type keyboard. It is a single unit occupying a discreet 10- by 14-inch space on the desk or table. It was developed by Matra, the French aerospace conglomerate, in a far-reaching experiment to provide businesses and households in France with an alternative to the telephone and telephone directory. Like the RCA,

Scanset has several shortcomings, even for the user who is interested only in accessing information services. It has no filing system and therefore cannot store information it receives from, say, Dow Jones. However, it can transfer information to a printer. Its keyboard is awkward and unsuitable for word processing, including the typing of electronic mail.

I think it is priced too high, but it does provide a simple way of tapping into the world of electronic information. Scanset is distributed in the United States by Tymshare, Inc., of Cupertino, California.

TEXAS INSTRUMENTS   Offering both a PC and a PC XT, Texas Instruments is a head-on 16-bit competitor with IBM. It is several hundred dollars less expensive than IBM and a generally better machine with a much better keyboard. However, it cannot run IBM software and suffers for that. A standard system comes with 128K of RAM expandable to 768K, two drives, detached keyboard and 12-inch monochrome display for $3,070. It is manufactured by Texas Instruments of Dallas, Texas.

ZENITH Z-100   A high-performance, well-regarded machine, which is in fact two computers in one. It has CP/M software on its 8-bit microprocessor and IBM-compatible software on its 16-bit processor. It comes in a wide variety of configurations, and a 128K system, expandable to 768K, with monochrome monitor, software, dual disk drives, built-in printer and modem hookups, and attachable keyboard has a list price of $3,599, but has been discounted as low as $2,815. In addition, Zenith provides an almost unprecedented 90-day, on-site free service to support this unit. This is a quality system at a bargain price.

Whatever system you choose, both hardware and software may prove a disappointment unless you know your needs and plan your purchases accordingly. Write out a list of what you want the system to do. After that, begin looking around.

But be careful. If you think the hookers at Times Square are on the make, wait until you start buying a computer. I hate to harp on the subject, but there are a lot of folks out there who'll try to pick your pockets clean. It's like a disease spread across the industry, but particularly noticeable at the consumer end—software manufacturers who won't correct mistakes after taking your money; magazines that whore themselves for advertisers and won't print uncomplimentary reviews of products; and computer-store salesmen who out of either ignorance or dishonesty always try to sell customers the highest-priced items, regardless of needs.

Not everybody, of course, is like that. But there are enough sleazes in the industry to make it worth your while to read the next chapter.

CHAPTER 6

Buyer Beware

I RECENTLY BOUGHT both a new car and a new computer system and the similarity of the experiences was depressing. Virtually every scam that was developed during the 80-year history of the automobile industry has been transported lock, stock and barrel to the personal computer industry.

There is the "low-ball," where the salesperson quotes a low price to snare the customer, then begins adding the options. Many a victim has gone into a computer store expecting to spend $1,795 on a system only to leave the store after signing up for $4,000, which is what is needed for the cables and boards and software and monitors and other peripherals necessary for the system to run.

Then there is the "waiting list," where you fork over a hefty deposit for the honor of being next on the waiting list for an in-demand computer or car. You will find that later comers—in-laws of the management, people willing to pay a bonus for quick delivery, stunning blondes, rock stars and drinking buddies—will be getting immediate delivery while you're still on the waiting list.

And there is the "gone and forgotten" service policy. Once you are gone with your computer, you are forgotten in terms of service. They don't know you. All that sales attention that was lavished on you as a potential buyer is now transferred to other potential buyers.

RIPOFF TIPOFF I

When you buy a piece of computer hardware or software and open the box, you're likely to find a document with something like this printed on it:

LIMITED WARRANTY

This program, instruction manual and reference materials are sold "as is." The entire risk as to the results and performance of the hardware/software is assumed by you. In no event will we be liable for any direct, incidental, indirect, special or consequential damages in connection with this product, [etc.]

It's a divorce from responsibility rarely found in the business world. Can you imagine buying a car or television set or kitchen appliance and being told that, no matter what happens, it's your problem?

Nevertheless, such warranties are a norm in the software business and occur more often than I'd like in the hardware business.

A growing number of judges and juries have decided that such warranties have no legal existence. If a salesman sells you a product and states it will do a particular job, then the product must match the job or the consumer has a right to a refund, or to a product that will do what the salesman claimed.

It doesn't matter what any subsequent disclaimer says, the representation has already been made about the product. To the extent that the representation is why you bought it, that is the basis of the contract. False advertising, say the courts, can't be remedied by a warranty disclaimer.

The warranty is basically a bluff, an intimidator put out by the company in hopes that it will discourage buyers from taking further action.

This chapter, therefore, will attempt to provide the following advice:

· How to locate a trustworthy vendor.

· How to negotiate a fair price for a system.

· How to buy additional peripherals and software.

· How to replenish consumable supplies such as disks, printer ribbons and printer paper.

Let's not fool ourselves that any of this is going to be easy. It's not easy to buy. And once you get the stuff, some of it will be damned difficult to use. But the investment of your time here will save much money and many headaches later on.

How to Select a Trustworthy Vendor

This may be the most important part of the task of buying a computer.

One thing to remember about computer salespeople is that more than 90 percent of them are new to the business. Their ignorance of a new industry is understandable. And it isn't necessarily their ignorance that can cost you. It is their refusal to admit ignorance.

Most of the salespeople also work on commissions. That means they have an interest in selling you the highest-priced goods.

But if you look hard, you will find here and there honest stores staffed with honest people who give good advice and good value. Unfortunately, to get to those people you may have to run an ungodly gauntlet of holdup men and con artists who will pick your pockets clean and laugh while doing it, unless you protect yourself.

To do that, here is some practical advice:

1. Before you even approach a store or mail-order house, write a letter stating in simple language what you want the product to do. This letter is for your own guidance. And a copy should be given to the salesperson you are dealing with.

2. Inform yourself by reading books and magazines, by talking with friends and particularly by talking with "user's groups" who are familiar with the functions you need—whether it be a $110 telecommunications software package or a $4,000 computer that will handle your inventory and bill customers.

3. Begin visiting stores. Check the yellow pages and the newspaper ads and make a list of the stores in your area. Browse around. Pay attention

Visit Stores

to the conversations between sales personnel and other customers. You'll soon know if you want to do business in that store or not.

4. Make notes on both the stores you visit and the conversations you have with sales personnel. If they offer a price on a system, ask them to write down the components and prices. After you've gathered up several of these lists, you can compare offers at home without pressure.

Have Conversations
with the
Sales Personnel

5. Make an appointment after you've decided what you want and which stores you might safely deal with. The appointment allows the store to assign a salesperson who knows about your product. If you just walk in and take the first salesperson available, chances are high that he will know no more about the product than you do.

6. Be patient. You'll probably get more attention, more courtesy and far more expertise from your butcher than from the average computer salesperson.

Be Patient

Don't Be Intimidated

7. Don't be intimidated by jargon. Bring along this book or a paperback dictionary of computer terms. If the salesperson uses a word you don't understand, ask for an explanation in English. If they can't provide it, have them show it to you in the glossary or dictionary.

8. Bring along a consultant. This doesn't have to be a paid professional. Knowledgeable friends, including blood relatives and spouses, can provide invaluable help. They can stand back and observe while you and

JARGON

If you demand detailed and realistic images in what finally appears on your computer screen, ask about pixels. These are the smallest picture elements on a computer screen, each literally a dot, and are a measure of screen resolution.

In computer terminology the word "bug" means an error. And when salespeople talk about booting the machine, they are not talking about kicking or hitting the computer. To boot means to start up a computer program.

An RS-232C is a type of computer connection. If your computer has an RS-232C serial interface, or "port," it means it can be used with a modem.

the salesperson are concentrating on each other. If you can't bring a knowledgeable friend, hire a professional. They charge between $15 and $75 an hour and average about $20 an hour. A good consultant's advice can save far more than your fee.

Finding the names of such consultants isn't always easy. Some may be listed in the yellow pages. But you are more likely to find them through the local computer clubs.

9. Don't be afraid to check backgrounds. There may come a time when you are close to a purchase and everything seems right except that you have a queasy feeling about the dealership. Check out the store. This isn't always easy, even with retailers located in your own city. The Better Business Bureaus reflect only the most flagrant cases of consumer abuse. Consumer protection agencies do a little better job but still tend to protect all but the most egregious offenders.

The most practical source of information about the integrity and performance of a retailer is the public record. First, call the state agency that handles corporate records and learn the legal identity of the retailer. Some companies do business under one name and incorporate themselves under another. Then call the local county courthouse and check for small claims and civil suits filed against the retailer. One or two claims may not be significant. Anyone can have disagreements. More than that should be a definite warning signal. In the case of a mail-order house, check the home courthouse of the retailer.

10. As an alternative to thorough background checks, ask for references. Stores that provide good service are pleased to provide the phone numbers or addresses of customers, individuals and companies that are will-

ing to be contacted as references. If the store won't provide references, then go somewhere else. Quick.

Negotiating a Fair Sale

If you follow the above preparations, you'll probably end up with two or three stores which you can trust. The next step is to get a fair price and decent sale conditions from one of the good stores. Here are some ways to do that:

1. Check your newspaper ads and see if any stores in the area are selling a system similar to the one you want. Chances are high that over a three- or four-week period one of the sleazeball stores in your area will advertise a very low price. You don't want to deal with those stores, of course, but it gives you a bargaining platform to use with the good stores.

    The discount price still represents a profit to the seller. Phone the good stores and ask if they are willing to match it. Usually they will, particularly in the sale of entire systems.
2. If none of the good stores are willing to meet the advertised discount prices, ask each one to give you a price on the system.
3. Visit the store that gave you the lowest phone quote and ask for a written list of the system components and their prices. If you are satisfied with that price, go ahead with your purchase.
4. However, if you think you can still beat the price, take the written list to the other good stores. Many times they will change their mind when they see you are ready to buy.
5. Never pay cash. If possible, always pay by credit card. Even if the store adds three or four percent to your bill for using the credit card, the extra protection probably is worth it. The reason some retailers insist on cash isn't to avoid paying a percentage to the credit-card company. It's to finesse you out of some very real but little-known consumer protection rights.

    Under federal law, use of a credit card in effect gives the consumer a 90-day warranty. Anytime within 90 days of purchase, the consumer can instruct the credit-card company to withhold payment or retrieve payment; you can cancel the portion of the payment that is in dispute and follow up with a letter to the credit company and the retailer explaining the nature of the dispute. If there is no agreement at the end of 90 days, the credit-card company steps back, cancels all payments, and the matter is left to settle between the consumer and the retailer. But the consumer at that point has paid no money.

6. If you do pay cash, or by check, and there is a dispute, then contact the consumer protection agencies or the BBB. They shine at negotiating such disputes without having to go to court.

7. Keep all copies of all documents: receipts, manuals and particularly advertising material. You never know when you're going to need them. Write everything down. When you complain, put it in writing. It's okay to phone, but follow it up with a letter. That way, a file has to be opened by the retailer. Save everything.

8. Try always to get a written agreement in the sales contract or receipt stating that you can return the system within 30 days, no ifs, ands or buts. When you get the system installed in your home or office, push it hard for that 30 days.

9. Ask about where you can go to get technical help after purchase. Is there an 800 number you can call if you have a question or a problem? An 800 number is a definite plus.

Buying Software and Peripherals

A microcomputer without software is like a record player without records. Unfortunately, the state of the industry makes buying software far more difficult than picking out the latest Michael Jackson hit. It is as if each record-player manufacturer designed its turntables to spin at different speeds and hold records of different sizes. To work, programs must be tailored to specific computer models.

The situation is further complicated by differences in systems software. As I mentioned earlier, each microcomputer contains an operating system (called DOS, for Disc Operating System), a program that controls the way in which the various pieces of the computer system communicate with one another. DOS regulates how information from the keyboard is processed, drives the video display, reads and writes information to and from the computer's disk storage and runs the modem and printer.

The same computer will run differently with different operating systems. Some computers come equipped with more than one operating system and many can be adapted to run more than one DOS.

The first step in selecting software or peripherals (hardware additions to your system) is to decide exactly what you want to use them for. That may seem obvious, but you'd be surprised at the number of people who buy hardware and software with only a vague idea of exactly how they will use it.

The cost of computer software varies greatly. Some electronic bulletin boards offer "freeware" of various sorts for the cost of copying the program. Commercial business-accounting packages, at the other extreme, can run into thousands of dollars.

Generally the price of programs is pegged to the cost of the computers that run them. Just as the microcomputer market is breaking up into three categories—home computers for $100 to $1,000, personal computers for $1,000 to $5,000 and small-business computers for $5,000 to $10,000—so is the associated software market. A competent communications program for a $300 home computer will range from $50 to $100. For a more expensive personal or business system, the cost of a similar, but more sophisticated, package will run between $150 and $1,000.

Because computers are so flexible, different programs can use remarkably varied and sometimes extremely arbitrary methods to accomplish a given task. This means that intuition is of little help in figuring out how a program should work, even for the experienced user. So the quality of the instruction manuals is of critical importance.

A useful rule of thumb in shopping for software is to look over the instruction manuals carefully and rule out programs with inadequate documentation.

The first thing to look for is an index. If the manual doesn't have an index, chances are high that the manual is inferior. A table of contents is no substitute for an index. God knows the number of labor hours that have been spent by people pawing through non-indexed manuals looking for information they need.

In addition to an index, a good manual will have a tutorial section that takes the user step by step through specific examples that show how the program works. And it will have a glossary of all its commands.

There are thousands of programs now on the market. Unless you are shopping for an expensive system, don't expect salespeople to spend much time with you. And don't expect them to know what they're talking about.

After Mary and I bought our first micro, an Apple II Plus, I was interested in adding telecommunications ability so that I could send and receive messages. It would be particularly helpful in communicating with my editors in New York. I knew very little about the subject except that one needed a thing called a modem and another thing called a communications program.

So I went to three computer stores to seek advice. Salespeople in each of the stores knew exactly what I needed and each strongly recommended a specific software package. None, however, recommended the same piece of software.

Indeed, the main thing that the packages had in common was that each was the highest-priced item of its kind in the store. They ranged from $350 to $750. A modem would cost me another $350 or more. And I'd also need a serial card, an interface that would connect the computer to the modem. That would add another $150. Even at the cheapest store, the total price was close to $1,000.

I decided to wait until I knew more about the subject.

A month later, after talking with friends and a lot of reading, I bought a Hayes Micromodem II through a mail-order house for $225. That price included everything.

I now know that the Hayes Micromodem is the best known of all modems and is considered the best modem for the Apple II series because it comes with a serial card built in. It also comes with its own communications program.

I learned that two of the three stores I visited had the Micromodem in stock at the time I was there. The salespeople were simply trying to gouge me.

Other novice buyers run the same risk. They can put themselves blindly in a salesperson's hands to have their pockets picked. Or they can educate themselves.

There are several inexpensive ways to do the latter. You can always turn to that knowledgeable friend for advice. You can attend a meeting or meetings of local computer clubs and get advice. People at such clubs are friendly and willing to share experiences and advice. The pooling of information is the reason the clubs were formed in the first place. Not only will you learn about hardware and software but you'll learn which stores and salespeople to avoid. How to find such clubs? Call your local newspaper's business editor, for a start. Or call a computer store. A quality store will know. If they don't know, you've learned something about the store.

You can read. Read what? Everything. Books. Magazines. Newspaper articles. Bulletin boards, once you're on line.

BRAVE NEW WORLD

For trivia buffs: The fastest computer printer in the world can print 45,000 lines per minute. It can print the five-million-word, 2,055-page *Random House Dictionary of the English Language* in 13 minutes. Know what it's used for? Junk-mail advertising.

Each medium has its pluses and minuses. Books on specific subjects should give you a more thorough background than other media. But, by their nature, they will not contain the latest information on specific products or services. Books are good tutors but slow reporters.

Newspaper articles bring the freshest news. They are good for breaking news, such as an announcement by IBM that it is introducing a new series. Newspapers are generally poor in background information, however, and their writers often show an appalling ignorance of the subject. This is understandable. Few newspapers have "computer" reporters. The reporters and editors tend to be all-purpose types. But the reader doesn't know this, and a lot of simply bad information gets repeated as a result.

On the other hand, computer magazines *do* have reporters and editors who are knowledgeable about computers. Most of these magazines are quite informative and trustworthy, for what they say. It's what they don't say that hurts. Many consumer magazines suffer from boosterism. They are so blindly positive about the industry and their advertisers that it amounts to a fraud against their readers. In general, the best parts of such magazines are (1) their ads and (2) their letters column.

The ads give you a quick, colorful look at what's new in the market. And the letters are where you will find real, honest opinions expressed. The letter writers are wonderful. They denounce the products and companies that are bad and they praise the ones that are good. Companies frequently respond. It's a marvelous bulletin board.

And let me add that there are magazines which are trustworthy and which print tough and fair reviews. Among these are *Interface Age, Peelings, Popular Computing* and *Creative Computing.*

One of the best is *InfoWorld,* a news weekly for microcomputer users that is available at newsstands and bookstores. Each issue has at least six software reviews. For $3.95 *InfoWorld* will send you its Report Card, a detailed evaluation of more than 50 of the most popular software packages and brief summaries of over 250 others.

Replenishing Supplies

There will be weeks when it seems that you spend more time and money equipping a computer than running data through it. Furthermore, it is a law of nature that the day you run out of some supply is always the day you need it in a rush and every supplier in town is out of stock. Small wonder. With over 200 different computer-printer ribbons on the market, for example, who can stock them all?

RIPOFF TIPOFF II

When you start buying software, you're going to see some things you won't believe. For example, as I write this I am looking at a $100 software package which reads:

"This diskette remains the property of [the manufacturer]. It is licensed to the purchaser for personal use only. This diskette may not be copied or used for any commercial purpose without the express written permission of [the manufacturer]."

Another piece of software in my office says that by opening the package I have agreed to the "licensing conditions."

Those items were sent to me for review. I wouldn't have bought them under any circumstances. What they are saying is that I have paid my money but I haven't bought anything.

Well, take it easy. Don't be misled by such "license agreements." According to a growing number of lawyers specializing in computer-consumer law, software that is "licensed" is in fact sold to you and not licensed.

The licensing "agreements" are contrary to a whole body of law in that one of the main attributes of a sale is that it gives the buyer full domain over the property.

A favorite "licensing" device is the self-executing one which says that when you break the seal or open the package you are deemed to have accepted the manufacturer's terms. That is a lot of bull, according to attorney L. J. Kutten of St. Louis, Missouri.

Such tactics have been tried before in the automobile industry and have been regularly ruled illegal by the courts, says Kutten, whose book, *The Computer Buyer's Protection Guide,* published by Prentice-Hall, is worth having on your bookshelf.

If you need it today, good luck. But there are dozens of mail-order houses which will get you the stuff you need within 48 hours via United Parcel Service's Blue Label express service. If you need it tomorrow, they'll express it overnight at higher cost. Mail-order houses are the best way to shop for supplies that you plan to keep in inventory.

There are dozens of aggressive marketers throughout the country who sell computers using a double whammy of well-stocked warehouses and well-manned telephones tied to 800 numbers. Some of their ads emphasize low prices, some fast service and some huge inventories. But they all compete against one another on all three fronts, which is a major break for large and small buyers of computer supplies.

From them, I've received printer ribbons in two days by United Parcel Service and bulkier supplies, such as printer paper, within five days.

The most economical way to buy computer supplies is to order before an emergency hits. That way you can shop for the best price and ship via the cheapest route.

The mail-order houses stock more than just ribbons and paper and disks. Most also sell furniture, file equipment, computer printers, cables, forms-handling equipment, modems and switches for linking several computers to peripheral equipment.

I like to browse through catalogs when they arrive to see what's new. For example, did you know that you can order letterheads and business forms custom-printed on computer paper?

From one supplier, I order stationery-quality paper which is perforated so closely that each sheet rips loose from its tractor-feed margins with scarcely a trace of the rough edges common to most computer print-outs.

From another supplier, I order windowed envelopes which allow me to print addresses, return addresses and a letter on a single sheet of paper. There's no need to address envelopes separately, either directly or with labels.

It's important to compare prices on everything everywhere, including your local stores, which sometimes will undersell mail-order houses because they want to clear their inventory.

Most mail-order suppliers stock their own private-label disks at bargain prices. I'd advise against buying them, however, to avoid any risk of bugs. The disks are the most important accessory in any system. Stick to brand names.

Large quantities of an item are often lower priced. In fact, if you keep records of how much you use of all consumable supplies, you may be able to save a lot by buying a year's worth at a time. Name-brand disks, for example, sell much more cheaply when bought in lots of one hundred. That sounds like a lot of disks, but you can split the order up among friends. Disks that retail at $3.90 each often sell for $1.90 each when purchased in lots of one hundred. That's a saving of $2.00 per disk.

The trick to buying ribbons is to order a minimum quantity first. Catalog houses all buy from a number of ribbon-winders and quality varies greatly from batch to batch. So buy a few and if they're good, quickly reorder a large lot from the same batch. But don't order more than you can use in six months. They deteriorate.

As the good old police sergeant on *Hill Street Blues* used to say, "It's a jungle out there. So let's be careful."

CHAPTER 7

The First Call

ONCE THE computer, modem and communications software are hooked up and working together, the system is said to be "up and running."

We are ready to make the first call. There are two questions: how to do it and whom to call.

For that very first time on line with a data base, it would be nice to call a base that would test your system and abilities without disturbing a local bulletin board or making a long-distance call.

This call can be made to Tymnet, the packet network that has toll-free phone facilities in most cities. Here's how:

1. Find a Tymnet 800 number, usually 800-538-5465 or 800-336-0149. (If in doubt, because the number may vary depending upon your area code, call the 800 information operator at 1-800-555-1212 and ask for a Tymnet number.)
2. Load your communication program into your terminal.
3. Turn on the terminal and set its switches to 'full duplex' and 'on line,' for remote session.
4. Dial your local Tymnet telephone access number and wait for a high-pitched tone.

5. If you have an acoustic coupler, place the telephone handset firmly in the coupler, orienting it in the direction indicated.

6. If you have a direct-connect modem, your communications program will indicate when a connection is established.

7. If you have a 300-Baud modem, there should be no problem. If your modem or terminal operates only at 1,200 Baud, you must use specific telephone numbers for access. You may obtain these from Tymnet.

8. When you have connected to the network, Tymnet will display a request for your terminal identifier. The message may appear garbled at a terminal operating at a speed other than 30cps (300 Baud). If so, don't worry about it. Wait a few seconds and type your identifier. (See step 9.)

9. Enter your terminal identifier character. (For these test purposes, the capital letter A will do.)

10. Tymnet will display some letters, the purpose of which doesn't concern this test, and then follow with a request to log in. The display should look something like this:

-NNNN-PPP-
please log in:

11. Type the word **INFORMATION;** ("Information" in caps followed by a semicolon) and hit a carriage return or **ENTER** key.

12. Tymnet will prompt (ask) for your password. Type the password given you by Tymnet, then hit the carriage return. A recent public password, for example, was **SUN2SHINE.** Passwords are not echoed back to your terminal for security reasons.

13. Tymnet will display an acceptance message such as a semicolon(;) or "host is on line," to indicate that you are connected to the host computer.

14. You are now on line. You should see the following display:

ITEM	FILE NAME	DESCRIPTION
1	@STATE	*Tymnet domestic access numbers by state*
2	@TYMSAT	*Tymnet public Tymsats sorted by node #*
3	@CITY	*Tymnet domestic access numbers by city*
4	@NEWPHONES	*Domestic access numbers for cities added during the last 90 days*
5	@CHANGEPHONES	*Changed and new access numbers for cities already on the Tymnet network*
6	@INTLPRT1COM	*Info on Tymnet international access*

ITEM	FILE NAME	DESCRIPTION
7	@CONFIG	*Configuration of Tymnet's international access*
8	@DPACACCESS	*DATAPAC access numbers*
9	@HOWTOUSETymnet	*Basic how to use Tymnet guide*
10	@BLUSEARCHCOM	*Computer and Data Services Available Through Tymnet (The BLUEBOOK)*
11	@BLUEINDEX	*Key-word index to the Computer and Data Services (Item 10)*
12	@DATAPACTymnet	*Logging in from DATAPAC to Tymnet*
13	@TymnetDATAPAC	*Logging in from Tymnet to DATAPAC*
14	@PCFILE	*Personal Computer Software Certified Operational on Tymnet*
15	@X25FILE	*X.25 PRODUCTS CERTIFIED BY Tymnet*

Tymnet will ask you to choose the information you would like from the menu by number. Browse through Tymnet until you feel comfortable with your system. You can't hurt Tymnet and it can't hurt you. Don't worry about the time spent on line. Tymnet considers it good public relations, which it is. When finished, type STOP to abort an unwanted listing; or QUIT to get out of the system. All input must be in CAPITAL letters.

After practicing on Tymnet you might want to try a local bulletin board, thus again avoiding long-distance charges. A bulletin-board system, also called a public access message system (PAMS), is what it sounds like: a message center open to all who can find it. The main difference is that instead of walking up and tacking on or reading a notice, you dial it on the computer. You can obtain a number from the appendix in the back of this book. You should choose several phone numbers because most bulletin boards can handle only one call at a time and the lines are frequently busy. A local Bulletin Board System (BBS) often has no sign-on fee and carries a list of other bulletin boards in your city or area code. Because phone numbers and bulletin boards change, the on-line list you obtain will be more current than the list in the back of this or any other book.

There are more than 1,500 bulletin boards nationwide. Most are free, and the ones that charge don't charge very much. The person who runs a bulletin board is called a sysop, systems operator. Most are volunteers. Some, however, are agents of computer dealers and publishers who use part of the board to peddle their wares.

Regardless of the sysop's motive, the boards are great community gathering places. Usually at no more cost than a local telephone call, you can send mail, gather news of interest, sell or buy items, obtain free computer programs and get help on technical problems.

Approximately 75 percent of the boards operate on restricted hours, usually after 8 P.M. when the sysop can break free of business and family duties to tend to the board. The sysop's presence, however, isn't necessary because the system is fully automatic. About a fourth of the systems operate 24 hours a day.

Sysop Directing Traffic

The systems are usually set up by the sysops as hobbies akin to ham radio operations. It costs money. To run a typical board, a sysop is essentially loaning a computer system to the world. Indeed, when you access a bulletin board, you are actually running the sysop's computer.

The board must include hundreds of kilobytes of on-line data storage and often includes several megabytes of hard-disk storage. Also required is a modem capable of answering the phone and a software program capable of operating the system.

The phone line also is loaned and the operator will put in many hours a week to keep the system running. Some hobby. But God bless them for their generosity.

Most of the boards will request the caller to enter his name, city and state, and phone number. This is to keep track of who the callers are and where they're calling from. It's part of the fun for the sysop. Though most people use their real names, at least initially, nicknames such as the Flying Phantom, Sun Man, Pretty Mama and the like are common.

Almost always, the board will ask for a password or identification code. New callers are assigned one after their identity is verified by the sysop.

Some boards have security levels that provide users with access to various parts of the board. The higher the security level, the greater the access to privileged information. At the very lowest security, however, callers can read and post messages and exchange electronic mail with other users.

Here is an example of a local, noncommercial board in Miami. To call up your board on line, first configure your system to the following parameters:

Full duplex	**7-bit character length**	**Stop bit: 1**
300 Baud	**Parity: even**	**Echo: On**

If your communications program doesn't ask you to enter any or all of the above parameters, don't worry about it. The setting, which is standard, is probably already built into the program. Sometimes either your communications program or the bulletin board itself will ask you how many "nulls" you need. A null is a control character sent by the remote computer to slow transmission speeds. In these examples it is used when you set up your printer to print information as it comes across the screen. The delay is necessary because the print head on a printer needs time to return to the left margin to print the next line.

If you're not using a printer on line, enter zero as the number of nulls needed. If using a printer, you'll need between one and 50 nulls. Since each brand of printer moves at a different speed, you'll have to experiment to find the necessary nulls.

Finally, and let me emphasize this, don't worry if anything goes wrong. If you are on line and things glitch or strange emblems appear on the screen, not to fret. There is nothing, nothing, that you can do from the keyboard that will hurt your system or the system you are calling.

So here goes. The example that follows is from a typical board. Pay attention to the command listings. They in fact are a catalog of the many features offered by the system.

STEP ONE Dial the local access number and wait for your communications software to inform you that you have established a connection. If you are listening on the handset, you will hear a high-pitched squeal. If you are simply watching the display screen of your monitor, you will see the other computer announce itself.

STEP TWO When the connection is made, hit **RETURN** or **ENTER** twice, then follow this sequence:

WHAT YOU SEE	WHAT YOU TYPE
Call number 1493 1200-Baud supported Welcome to YOUR BBS	(*This is the bulletin board announcing itself*).
User number or N for new? Press ⟨Enter⟩ or ⟨CR⟩ to abort	*N*
Enter name: Enter phone number Enter password choice:	*DAVID CHANDLER* (*XXX-XXX-XXXX*): *TEST*
Is this correct?	*Y*

Your user number is: KA8

New users will be verified by mail only. Send a letter to the system operator (address later) and include the user number and password you entered.

Inactive users are purged from the system once a month. If you have not accessed for a month or more, your password will be deleted. Also, if the phone number you entered at the time you first signed on is found to be an invalid one, your entry will be dropped. Phone numbers entered on the system are considered confidential and are not given out to anybody without your permission.

The use of obscene or otherwise objectionable language is not allowed in any part of the public sections. Users who use such language will be dropped from the system and a public message posted with their names and an explanation of the reason.

Commands:

⟨B⟩ulletins Displays general interest notices about the System.

⟨D⟩ownload Allows downloading of binary files. User must be using a compatible program.

WHAT YOU SEE	WHAT YOU TYPE

⟨E⟩nter Allows verified users to enter public messages. Unverified users can only leave private messages to the system operator.

⟨F⟩leamarket Allows posting of buy/sell ads. Ads will be read in a last-in-first-out order.

⟨G⟩raffiti A section for short messages. Messages in this section are usually fast paced and sometimes quite unique. Topics will vary very quickly.

⟨H⟩elp Displays this listing.

⟨L⟩og Displays a listing of the last few users with the times and date of access.

⟨M⟩ail Private mail system. Verified users only, but a letter can be left to the sysop by a new user.

⟨N⟩ewsletter General Interest technical bulletins about computers in general or programming techniques that might be helpful to all.

⟨O⟩ff Logs user off the system.

⟨P⟩assword Allows a user to change his/her password. It is fully prompted.

(Note: A "prompt" is a symbol or word from the computer asking a question.)

⟨R⟩ead Displays messages in the public section of the board. ⟨S⟩kip and ⟨P⟩ause are active at the end of all lines except the header.

⟨T⟩ime Displays the time the user has been on the system. A maximum of 25 minutes per call is allowed to all callers. There is no limit on the number of calls a user can make.

⟨?⟩ Displays a short table of commands.

Unverified users do not have access to any of the sections that allow the

WHAT YOU SEE	WHAT YOU TYPE

posting of public messages. These sections are only available for reading.

Do you want to log off?

Thank you for using YOUR BBS
Time on System 00:07:13

These bulletin boards are run on computers in people's homes or in small computer stores. Most have a theme. Some are oriented to users of a particular computer, such as an Apple or IBM. Others carry personal messages. Some are political. Some are interested in swapping technical information. Each board carries its own command structure. And most are quite easy to understand.

Regardless of system orientation, they are phoned by all kinds of computers. The users of local boards amount to a sort of club, and you can attend club meetings every night without leaving your house.

Once you've reached your first bulletin board, finding others will be easy. Boards list one another's phone numbers, particularly in the same city.

The hard part is finding that first number. One means is via the commercial information services such as CompuServe or The Source. Most purchasers of modems and communications software receive a membership in CompuServe or The Source either free or for a small cost. Those two systems each carry extensive lists of bulletin-board numbers throughout the United States and in some possessions and territories, such as Guam and Puerto Rico.

When researching bulletin boards, you'll notice that many use names like Net-Works and ABBS. This is a reference to the software used by the board system. Net-Works, from High Technology of Oklahoma City, is one of the most popular boards. In addition to public and private mail exchange, the Net-Works system allows Apple users with a Hayes Micromodem II to obtain software programs directly from the bulletin board.

Another popular board is ABBS, for Apple Bulletin Board System, made by Software Sorcery of McLean, Virginia. ABBS boards generally have more features than Net-Works boards.

An even more elaborate system is PMS, People's Message System from Datel Systems of Lakeside, California. As a public service, Datel runs what is probably the world's largest listing of bulletin boards. It covers boards of all kinds of computers using all kinds of bulletin-board systems:

Downloading

IBMs, Apples, Zeniths, using ABBS, CBBS, Net-Works. A print-out of the listings would cover more than thirty pages. As a consequence, it is best to call up only those boards you are interested in, such as those grouped by area code or type of board system or type of computer.

Except for the long-distance tolls, PMS is a free service. You can call the board, located in Santee, California, by dialing 619-561-7277.

Type a question mark anytime you are unsure of what to do while using a board or virtually any data information base. The question mark is a universal SOS system for computer users.

Most bulletin boards have three main services: a public board, private mail and free software programs.

The public board is the part that everyone is allowed to read. Notices include items for sale, requests for help in playing games or general information on everything from the time the boat parade starts to whether anyone wants to swap software or buy a used lawn mower. It is common to find beginning and advanced computer-system users calling for help to solve a particular problem. You'll find teen-agers seeking help for Wizardry, baffled correspondents trying to learn how to deal with the intricacies of a printer, and jargonistic programmers talking about Static Storage Allocation and Synchronous Time Division Multiplexing.

The bulletin boards also serve as a library for free software, called "public domain" software because it has been donated to the computer community without copyright. Once you have been on a bulletin board several times you will learn from the individual system how to enter the host computer's operating system and obtain a list or catalog of all the software files on the host computer's disks.

The act of taking these files and transferring them to your own system is called "program downloading." If, as you should, you want at times to donate your own public domain software, you send it to the host computer in a process known as "program uploading." In other words, if you are taking the program, you are "downloading." If you are giving, you are "uploading."

Some of the sysops have high-capacity hard disks which offer hundreds of programs free for the taking. Many of the programs are quite useful and often are the direct equivalent of programs sold in stores at considerable sums.

While bulletin boards can be accessed by any type of communications system, downloading and uploading often require compatibility between operating systems. Thus, to get the most free programs, you will seek a bulletin board that uses the same operating system as you do. It is not a problem—there are numerous bulletin boards for each operating system all over the country.

Another board feature is private mail. Private mail is just that, although the sysop has access to anything sent to the board.

Private or restricted access also is kept by boards with specialized interests. An example of these is The Notebook, a board operated in Palm Beach, Florida, by two professional writers. They set up The Notebook as a bulletin board for professionals. Writers and photographers post their availability for assignments, and editors and publishers post notices when they are seeking journalists or particular articles.

It is a generous service and the sysops ask no fee. Frankly, I am glad these sysop types are around. It's time the nice people in America started coming out of the closet.

Downloaded

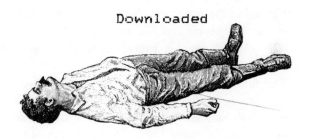

CHAPTER 8

Data for Hire

WE ARE NOW ABOUT TO MEET the commercial data bases, the ones that cost money to use. These are the information services that can give us the ball-game scores, the latest news, airline schedules, reviews of restaurants and hotels in distant cities, investment and other commercial information, and practical advice on how to use computers. These bases usually work beautifully. But for the novice, things sometimes go wrong. When they do, the user tends to get nervous because every minute on line costs money, either to the user or to whoever or whatever is paying the bill.

Particularly rattling are those times when the host computer gets "hung up." A command has been given to display airline schedules and nothing happens. The cursor vanishes. The meter ticks. The watcher waits. The screen doesn't move. Money drains into a bottomless pit.

I panicked the first time it happened to me. It was on a Sunday night. I was on The Source and had asked UPI News to give me the first paragraphs of all stories that had appeared in the past week concerning the space shuttle.

The cursor vanished, indicating to even my rookie mind that it had gone somewhere, that the computer was at work. But nothing happened. Just a green-on-black immobile screen staring back with the last words entered, "space shuttle."

After two minutes, which seemed like ten, I grabbed for The Source manual. Had I done something wrong? More minutes passed as I frantically thumbed through, eyes darting between the screen and the manual. I had done it right. But The Source wasn't moving.

Convinced it was broken, I tried to sign off. I hit **RETURN, ENTER, OFF, EXIT,** anything I could think of. None of it worked. I panicked and saw my hand, as if it were an independent thing, reach out and turn the computer off.

As it did so, I was thinking, My God, without a sign-off, The Source computer is going to think I am still on line and charge me a bundle.

I promptly phoned The Source's emergency 800 number to ask someone to sign me off officially.

There was no answer. I dialed again. Five, six, seven rings. No answer. And again. Then I checked the manual. The emergency folks didn't man the phones after midnight. I went to bed that night figuring I would need a lawyer to get out of this one.

I did phone the next day to see what I could salvage from the situation. The Source people said "Hey, no problem." Their computer automatically detects broken transmissions and signs off the caller.

All commerical data bases do that. So don't worry if things stall. If you can sign off, do so. It will save you the two minutes or so of cost that the computer will take to detect the broken transmission. But otherwise, just break the connection by shutting off the computer or hanging up the phone.

Some systems, such as the CompuServe data base, take as long as 20 minutes to detect a broken transmission. But even that is only two dollars (at CompuServe's standard rate of six dollars an hour). There will be times when the system "hangs." The whole operation seems to lapse into a reverie. The screen doesn't move. The cursor, if you can see it at all, doesn't blink. When that happens, there are three options:

One, stay with the system until it does something. It might be busy on a search and come back in minutes, or it might never come back. You take your chance.

Two, if you have two phone lines in your house, use the other line to call the data base's customer service number, which will be prominently displayed in the manual.

Three, break the connection by shutting off the computer or hanging up the phone.

Computers will hang, including the mainframes of the big data bases. One reason is a heavy work load. The more people connected at a single time to a data base, the slower it goes. You can feel the surge of new users coming on line if you are in an eastern time zone and happen to be on The Source or CompuServe when the rates change west of you at 7:00 P.M. The boards slow down and become sluggish.

An equally frequent cause of hangs and stalls, however, is poorly thought-out command procedures. For example, let's research the subject "promotion." If you are looking at it from a perspective of personnal management, you should search for the term "personnel and promotion" or "hiring and promotion."

If, on the other hand, you are looking for information on how to publicize or "promote" something, then use the term "public relations and promotion" or "advertising and promotion."

MONEY SAVER

Every minute spent on a commercial data base costs money, from several cents to several dollars. To reduce those costs by as much as 90 percent, beginners should always, repeat always, consult the system manual in advance and write down the command sequence. This should be done for the simplest chores, even checking for electronic mail on The Source.

Users new to a data base face many challenges. They can be overcome, however, with a little planning. The best way to get acquainted with a data base is to get it on line and then browse through it. The minute you begin to browse, however, the meter begins to tick. So, to get a sense of what the data bases look like we'll take a sightseer's tour of three general-purpose data bases. These will be The Source and CompuServe, the two largest and best known, and Delphi, a fresh and energetic newcomer.

All three data bases are accessed through three information gates: Telenet, Tymnet and Uninet. These gates were originally established so that banks and other financial institutions could exchange data through a central exchange that had a local telephone number. The gates were opened to the public when the personal computer market began to boom. If you live in a city, chances are high that you can access one or more of the gates by dialing a local number.

To obtain that local number, look in the phone book for "GTE Telenet," or "Tymnet" or "Uninet." If they aren't listed, dial 1-800-555-1212 and ask the AT&T information operator for the toll-free 800 number.

Here's a sample log-on sequence via Telenet to The Source. Don't try yet to do this yourself. Just follow me as I do it.

WHAT YOU SEE	WHAT I TYPE
TELENET	
305 13B	
TERMINAL=	*D1 (This is the terminal identifier for most personal computers.)*
@	*c 30138 (The "at" sign is Telenet's request for the Data Bank you are seeking. In this case, c 30138 is the number entered for The Source. The number was assigned to me by The Source and will vary depending on location and other factors.)*
c 301 38 CONNECTED	
Connected to THE SOURCE	
⟩ id	*STZ123 USER (The Source has asked for the password issued to me as a subscriber.)*
ST9502 (user 35) logged in Welcome, you are connected to THE SOURCE	
1 USING THE SOURCE 2 TODAY 3 BUSINESS UPDATE 4 THE SOURCE MAIN MENU 5 WHAT'S NEW 6 COMMAND LEVEL	
Enter item number or HELP	

At this point, The Source has offered its first menu. Item one gives a brief tutorial on using The Source. Item two is a sort of daily almanac entry complete with famous birthdays. Item three gives the latest business news. Item four leads to the main menu of Source offerings. The menus are built like a tree, with the main-branch menu carrying you to different limbs, which in turn will carry you to smaller, more closely defined limbs until eventually you arrive at what you want. Item five gives information on late developments in using The Source. And item six allows you to by-pass the menu tree and go directly to what you want.

All three services open new opportunities for innovative business people. In addition to the obvious uses of stock market data and the like, consider these case histories:

1. Computer translations. For years, your company has been storing data
   on text files in a Radio Shack computer. The boss, however, has bought
   an Apple Lisa and naturally wants to have access to the company records.
   But the Radio Shack disks will not run on the Lisa. How do you translate
   the years of information? There are several solutions involving paying
   fees to commercial companies or consultants. If you are dealing exclusively in text files, however, a cheap and effective way out is to send
   the files to The Source as mail. Source mail is instantaneous and allows
   unlimited file length at low cost for storage. The boss simply dials The
   Source and picks it all up on the Lisa.

2. A New Orleans graphics designer bought 13 acres of woods and pasture
   land some 40 miles north of the city. He built a house, dug a fish
   pond, planted fruit trees and was realizing his lifelong dream of a peaceful
   place in the country. The one drag in his life was the two hours he
   spent each day commuting to and from his downtown office. Because
   he had a steady and profitable clientele, he decided he could close the
   office and work at home. He'd go into the city only for conferences.
   But he needed information on working at home. Were there tax disadvantages to consider? Or other pitfalls? He checked CompuServe, which
   keeps bulletin boards for nearly one hundred special interest groups
   (SIGs). Sure enough, CompuServe had a "Work-at-Home" SIG which
   allowed members to exchange information on the problems and advan-
   tages of working out of the home. Pilots, writers, doctors and other
   professionals also were represented by SIGs in order to confer with
   their peers. It is a simple matter to post a question one day and come
   back the next for your answers.

3. The manager of a small branch post office was considering whether
   or not to install a coin-operated copying machine. She had little guidance
   on which were the best brands. She decided to conduct a national survey
   by posting her questions on the bulletin boards of The Source and CompuServe. Both services have not only the bulletin boards but more formal
   mechanisms which allow surveys on a variety of subjects. The sampling,
   of course, will be skewed toward the type of people who use the information services. But in the manager's case it met her needs.

4. The boards also provide the equivalent of classified ads. If you have
   new or used equipment to sell, particularly if it is computer-related,
   post it on the board. Cars, boats, even homes have been sold.

5. Numerous companies use the information services to build mailing lists
   by compiling account numbers available on the utilities. They use the
   lists by sending out electronic mail flyers, price and service bulletins

and other material. The Source, for example, allows users to set up a permanent mailing list and then send a given message to all Source users on the list with a single command. CompuServe has no such bulk mailing system but can accomplish similar functions by sending to the aforementioned SIGs.

The main instruction from the above examples is that the commercial data bases can not only pay for themselves but actually earn money for those so inclined.

CHAPTER 9

The Source

I'D LIKE this service better if it didn't use a capital T in its title. But apart from that lapse in taste, this is my personal favorite of the general information systems. It offers something for everyone, from hard financial news to sports scores to bulletin boards to electronic mail.

It is one of the big three of the general information services, the others being CompuServe and Dow Jones News/Retrieval. The Source is the smallest of the three, having 41,000 members in early 1984 compared with 56,000 for CompuServe and 85,000 for Dow Jones.

The Source also is the most expensive to join. List price for a subscription is $100, compared with $19.95 for CompuServe and nothing for Dow Jones. In addition, The Source has a monthly minimum charge of $10 whether you use it or not. Neither CompuServe nor Dow Jones has a minimum.

Nevertheless, I find it worth the extra money. The subscription price is often reduced to zero when The Source is sold as part of another package. One of the communications programs I use, Transend I, sells for $89 and comes with a free Source membership.

You join The Source either as part of a package or by contacting them directly at:

Source Telecomputing Corporation
1616 Anderson Road
McLean, VA 22102
(800-336-3366)

The phone number is subject to change.

You will be issued a password, a user's identification number and a local access number connecting you to The Source via its own gateway, called Sourcenet, or through Telenet or Uninet.

Without further ado, let's log on:

STEP ONE Dial the local access number and wait for your communications software to inform you that you have established a connection.

STEP·TWO When the connection is made, hit **RETURN** or **ENTER** twice, then follow this sequence:

WHAT YOU SEE	WHAT YOU TYPE
TELENET 305 13B	
TERMINAL?	*D1 (The code for most personal computers.)*
@	*C 30138 (This figure has been given to you by The Source. It is its identifier number on Telenet. Telenet acts as a switchboard for hundreds of clients, and each, like The Source, has an identifier.)*
301 38 CONNECTED Connected to The Source	
⟩ id	*ZX7842 TEST (The Source has asked for your customer ID and your password. You enter both.)*

ST9502 (user 35) logged in.
Welcome, you are connected to The Source.

(C) COPYRIGHT Source
TELECOMPUTING CORPORA-
TION.
WELCOME TO The Source

1 USING The Source
2 TODAY

WHAT YOU SEE	WHAT YOU TYPE

---

3 BUSINESS UPDATE
4 The Source MAIN MENU
5 WHAT'S NEW
6 COMMAND LEVEL

Enter item number or help   *4 (The main menu).*

The Source MAIN MENU

1 NEWS AND REFERENCE RE-
SOURCES
2 BUSINESS/FINANCIAL MAR-
KETS
3 CATALOGUE SHOPPING
4 HOME AND LEISURE
5 EDUCATION AND CAREER
6 MAIL AND COMMUNICA-
TIONS
7 CREATING AND COMPUTING
8 Source*PLUS

Enter item number or help   *1 (We choose news, which leads to another menu.)*

NEWS & REFERENCE RE-
SOURCES

1 NEWS AND SPORTS
2 GOVERNMENT AND POLITICS
3 CONSUMER INFORMATION
4 BYLINES NEWS FEATURES

Enter item number or help   *3 (We choose item three and get:)*

CONSUMER INFORMATION

1 CONSUMER CORNER COLUM-
NISTS
2 BUYING WINE
3 RESTAURANT GUIDES

Enter item number or help   *3*

Let's say we're going to St. Louis and want to know about some restaurants. We select 3 and arrive at a data base of restaurants reviewed by the *Mobil Restaurant Guide.*

WHAT YOU SEE	WHAT YOU TYPE

RESTAURANT GUIDES

1 NATIONAL RESTAURANT
GUIDE
2 N.Y. CITY RESTAURANT
GUIDE
3 WASHINGTON RESTAURANT
GUIDE

Enter item number or help   *1*

A quicker way to get to restaurants is to bypass the menus and go into command mode as soon as The Source gives us its first menu.

WHAT YOU SEE	WHAT YOU TYPE

1 USING The Source
2 TODAY
3 BUSINESS UPDATE
4 The Source MAIN MENU
5 WHAT'S NEW
6 COMMAND LEVEL

Enter item number or help   *6 (The Source tells us we are at command level when it shows an arrow.)*

→   *USREST (US REST is the command to take us to the* Mobil Restaurant Guide *data base.)*

After we chose the Command Level, The Source gave us an arrow prompt (→) asking what data base we wanted. We typed **US REST** and went directly to the restaurant reviews, bypassing the menu trees and saving on-line time and money. We obtained the command **US REST** from a "guide book" which came with our Source membership package.

There are hundreds of separate programs and data bases on The Source. You can access any of these from Command Level by entering the program name at the → (arrow prompt).

Here are a few examples of programs accessed by entering their name at the →:

→ **STOCKVUE** Retrieves Media General's Stock Analysis service.
→ **USNEWS** Retrieves the weekly *U. S. Washington News Letter.*
→ **CSTORE** Retrieves the Comp-U-Store shopping service.

Sometimes a System Command should precede the program name, for example:

HELP Followed by a name retrieves background information on a data base, service or program. **HELP STOCKCHECK** retrieves program instructions and a demonstration.

PLAY Must be entered before the name of a game to begin play. **PLAY STARTREK** lets you play the game.

We'll now return to the restaurant data base. What follows is an actual on-line example. Watch for the mistakes.

WHAT YOU SEE	WHAT I TYPED
Enter City, State (for example, CHICAGO,IL:)	*St. Louis, Mo.*
State unknown.	*(????)*

This happened while writing this book. The Source told me that Missouri didn't exist.

I was reasonably sure that it did. I have been there several times. The Mississippi River flows by it. And my wife was born and raised there, or so she has always claimed. All of this indicated that "Mo." existed. The problem was to get agreement from The Source computer.

Computers, of course, are very literal. So I put Mo. in capital letters without spacing, as The Source had done with its example of Chicago. Again I got the line:

State unknown.

The Source then informed that I might have the wrong two-letter abbreviation for my state and instructed me to "list all" to get a listing of all the cities and states available. "List states" will provide you with a list of all the states and Canadian provinces covered by the restaurant guide, including their two-letter abbreviations.

I ran out the whole list and sure enough, Missouri was listed as "Mo." I tried all combinations of capital and lower-case letters, punctuation and spaces, no punctuation and no spaces.

I finally hit the right combination: (upper and lower case and no punctuation). Then The Source informed me:

The city "ST. LOUIS,MISSOURI" is not in the data base.

LOOKING FOR SAINT LOUIS

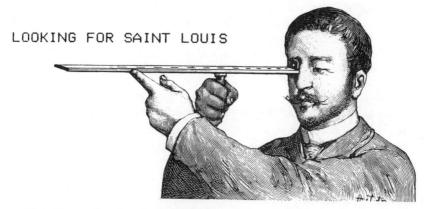

Now it was the city that had disappeared.

Once again I tried combinations. Upper case. Lower case. I even spelled it out: **SAINT LOUIS, MISSOURI.** The Source repeated:

the city "SAINT LOUIS,MISSOURI" is not in the data base.

Eventually I wrote, **St Louis,Mo**—no periods, no spaces between city and state. Then and only then did the computer agree.

34 restaurant(s) found in St Louis,Mo. 34 total.

I asked to see only the three-star restaurants. St. Louis, I was told, had 19 of them. Culling through, I narrowed my choice to two:

*** HENRY VIII. (4690 N Lindbergh Blvd, Bridgeton 63044) 731-4888. Hrs: 7 AM–11 PM; Sun to 9 PM. Closed Sun on hols. A/C. Continental menu. Bar, 10:30–1 AM. Semi-a la carte. Lunch, $3,25–$7.95; dinner, $11.95–$18.50 up. Child's plates half-price. Specializes in prime rib, Yorkshire pudding, Viennese pastries. Own baking. Background music. Pianist. Cr cds: A, C, D, MC, V. Wheelchairs. Spoken: German,French,Italian.

*** MISS HULLING'S.(Cafeterias) 11th & Locust St (63101), 8 blks W of I-55, I-70 exit Spruce or Chestnut Sts. 436-0840. Hrs: 6AM–8:15 PM. Closed Sun, most major hols (open Easter, Mother's Day, Father's Day on Sun). A/C. Bar. Bkfst. $2; lunch, $3.50; dinner, $4.50. Child's plates half price. Salad bar. Own baking. Background music. Cheerful garden atmosphere. Cr cds: A, D, MC, V. Wheelchairs.

Now that I had the system right, I called for Pocatello, Idaho, population 46,340. I have never been there but have always been intrigued by the name. The guide listed four restaurants, all with one star. The most interesting was:

* BUTTER BURRS. 917 Yellowstone Ave, 2 mi NE on US 91. 232-3296. Hrs: 7
AM–10 PM; Fri, Sat to 2 AM. Closed July 4, Thanksgiving, Dec 25. A/C. Semi-a
la carte. Bkfst, $1.25–$2.95; lunch; $1.95–$4.95; dinner, $2.65–$8.95. Child's plates.
Sr citizen rates. Specializes in homemade soups. Salad bar. Own baking, pastries,
breads. Background music. Cr cds: MC, V. Wheelchairs.

Sounds like Mom's good eats at good prices.

On a roll now, I picked out one of the smaller places I know, a community
nested in the beautiful Arkansas Ozarks and home of some of the finest
bluegrass music and moonshine whiskey in the world. I speak of the town
of Mountain View, population 1,966.

The only restaurant I could recall in Mountain View was a "Cafe and
Pool Hall" located across the street from the courthouse. But The Source
knew of another:

Restaurant(s) in Mountain View, AR

** OZARK FOLK CENTER. (See Ozark Folk Center Lodge) 264-3139. Hrs: 7
AM–9 PM. Closed Mon, Tu in May & Sep; also Nov–Apr; open wkends in Apr.
A/C. Southern menu. Semi-a la carte. Bkfst, $2–$4; lunch, dinner, $3.50–$9.75.
Child's plates, $1.65–$3.10. Specialties: country ham steak, chicken and dumplings,
ham and beans. Salad bar. Own baking. Background music. Cr cds: MC, V. Spoken:
Spanish.

I remember the place. It's actually a mile outside of town, in metropolitan
Mountain View.

The Source, of course, offers much more than restaurant reviews. It is
a world-wide information service accessible by virtually any microcomputer, terminal or communication word processor using a telephone and a
modem.

You can keep on top of unfolding news events, send mail electronically,
check airline schedules, arrange a trip, look in on the stock market and
analyze trends, chat electronically with others in the computer community,
play electronic games or shop.

A subsidiary of *Reader's Digest,* The Source operates through computer
telephone networks that link you to the mainframe computing power and
storage capacity of the company's mainframe computers in McLean, Va.

There are over 800 separate programs and data bases on The Source.
Many have different command procedures and those commands are listed
at the beginning of each program. There are two commands, however,
which are used in all Source programs. They are:

QUIT Entered at most prompts will take you to Command Level.
HELP Entered at a prompt will display instructions on that program.

ELECTRONIC MAIL

By the end of the century, two thirds of the nation's mail, or 140 billion postings a year, will be handled electronically. That is the conclusion of a study done by the Congressional Office of Technology Assessment, a federal agency with a very wide letterhead. OTA, as it abbreviates itself, says most of the mail will be handled by packet networks, such as Telenet, which currently offers Telemail. Mail will be transmitted from one computer to another.

Another form of electronic mail is sent electronically but delivered in hard copy. Western Union has such a service, called Mailgram, which has been operating since 1980.

A sparkling newcomer in the field is MCI Mail of Washington, D.C. It sends both electronic mail to computers and hard-copy mail to addresses. There is no sign-on charge, no monthly minimum and you get a free subscription to Dow Jones News/Retrieval when you join.

You pay only for the letters you send. You pay nothing for letters received. After you've signed up, you simply dial MCI on your computer and follow prompts to write your letter.

For $1, MCI delivers it almost instantly to any computer address you can give it. For $2, MCI will send a hard-copy letter to any physical address, via the Postal Service. For $6, MCI will hand-deliver it by noon the following day to addresses in some 20,000 locations in the contiguous 48 states. For $25, MCI will hand-deliver the letter within four hours to addresses in major cities.

I've used MCI for a year and like it.

MCI MAIL
Customer Service, Box 1001
1900 M Street, NW
Washington, DC 20036
(800-424-6677)

Here is a partial catalog of features offered on The Source, preceded by their program names:

ECOM   Electronic Computer-Originated first-class Mail service via the U.S. Postal Service and The Source.

ACCESS   The directory of all phone numbers used to connect to The Source via Sourcenet, Uninet and Telenet. Sign-on instructions for each network are included.

BIZDATE   Business and financial news, stock market and commodities indexes and prices—updated throughout the business day.

BULLETIN   When major news is breaking, type BULLETIN for the latest stories.

(PLAY) CASTLEQUEST   Search for treasure in the myriad rooms of the castle, a Dungeons and Dragons type of adventure game.

CURRENCY   Three daily updates of foreign exchange rates.

DOW   Dow Jones indexes, updated during trading.

(PLAY) EXPLORE   Search for treasure in a major metropolis.

GOLD   Latest status of gold trading world-wide.

METALS   Latest metal market activity from New York.

MICROLINE   Digital Research product information, press releases, trade show and seminar schedules, user groups and reference materials, questions and answers, independent software vendor information and more—updated weekly.

NYSE   New York Stock Exchange indexes, updated in session.

PARTI   The teleconferencing system PARTICIPATE, which allows multiple-party on-line conferences.

(PLAY) PITS   A new, enhanced version of the popular fantasy exploration game.

SP   Standard and Poor's hourly indexes.

SPORTS   Today's schedules and yesterday's results in baseball, football, hockey, soccer and basketball—and major stories.

STOCKCHECK   The latest stock-market quotes from United Press International.

TODAY   TV listings, horoscopes, feature stories, personalities, opinion forums and more.

UNISTOX   Daily money-market fund rates.

USCHAMBER   Daily Chamber of Commerce reports on congressional legislation affecting U.S. businesses.

USNEWS   The weekly *Washington News Letter* from *U. S. News & World Report.*

USROOM   *Mobil Travel Guide* rates 16,000 hotels, motels and inns in the continental United States and Canada.

ON-LINE PRINTING

Many people like to print the information they receive from The Source and other information services, concurrent with the display they see on the screen. They find, however, that they lose some of the words.

Here's why. The services' slowest transmission rate is 300 Baud. That comes out to about 30 characters per second. If the printer can't keep up with that speed, then characters are lost, usually one character out of ten.

These problems mostly arise in printers that use RS-232 serial interface cards. If the printer is connected via a parallel interface card, it probably will store a line at a time in a "buffer" before it prints the line. Since the process is fast, it is unlikely that any characters will be missed.

But don't despair if you use a serial interface. There is a solution. Use a telecommunication program, such as those described in chapter four. With those packages, incoming information can be read on the screen and afterward saved on a disk or other storage system. You can then print out the saved file at your convenience.

Another solution is to change the way you log onto the system. For Telenet, use the terminal identifier "A9" when Telenet says "Terminal=." For Tymnet, use terminal identifier "I" instead of "A" when it asks for terminal type. This will put enough delay between lines so that the printer can catch up before the next line starts coming in. But there is a trade-off. Your on-line time will increase significantly because of the delays.

The above barely scratches the surface. Almost daily, it seems, The Source adds and subtracts features. Here is a list of general subjects which can be found on The Source. The names of the programs containing information on these subjects can be found in The Source guide book that comes with your membership and is regularly updated. It can be found on The Source itself by entering the command **HELP LIBALL** (for Help Library ALL) after you've logged on and entered the command mode.

Bulletin Boards
Business News (updated throughout the day)
Business Publications Abstract Service
Business Calculations Programs
Business Services Index
Classified Ads
Commodity News

Currency Trading Quotes
Discount Shopping:
 General Merchandise
 Records and Tapes
 Classic Radio Programs
Dow Jones Hourly Indexes
ECOM Mail Message Service
Editorials (Syndicated Columnists)

Educational Programs and Drills
Employment Network
Finance:
 Personal Finance Programs
 Latest Stock Market Quotes
 Stock Market Reports
 Stock Performance Analysis
 Stock Portfolio Management
 New York Stock Exchange Indexes
 Standard and Poor's Indexes
 Dow Jones Indexes
 Metal Market Activity
 Gold Prices (Daily)
 Currency Trading Quotes
 Financial Modeling/Business Planning
 Financial Programming
 Business Finance Calculation Program
Games Library
Gold Prices (Daily)
Horoscopes
Hotel Guide (U.S. and Canada)
Mail
Mailgram Message Service
Metal Market Activity
Microcomputer News
Movie Reviews
Music To Order
News and Sports Service (United Press Int'l.)

Business News
News Bulletins
News Features
New York Stock Exchange Hourly Indexes
Personal Finance Programs
Research Service (Information On Demand)
Restaurant Guides:
 U.S. and Canada
Shopping Services:
 General Merchandise
 Records and Tapes
 Classic Radio Programs
 Book Ordering
Ski Reports (winter months only)
Sports Schedules and Scores
Stock Market—Latest Quotes
Stock Market Reports
Stock Performance Analysis (Media General)
Stock Portfolio Management
Travel Services:
 Airline Schedules
 Make Reservations
 Vacation Packages
TV Listings
U.S. Chamber Congressional Reports

To make things really easy, The Source markets a software disk called "Sourcelink" which allows sign-on with a single touch of a key and presents its programs in color. The touch of another button takes you directly to your data base of choice: news and sports, financial data, airline schedules.

ON-LINE RATES FOR
THE SOURCE

The Source offers approximately 800 information and communication services. The following charges are for the amount of time you actually are connected to The Source. Time is computed to the next nearest minute as recorded by computer. Connect-time charges are calculated as of *your* local time. There is a monthly minimum charge of $10. All prices are subject to change.

	300-BAUD SERVICE	1200-BAUD SER- VICE
Weekday 7:00 AM–6:00 PM	$20.75/hr.	$25.75/hr.
	$20.75/hr. Canada	$25.75/hr. Canada
	$20.75/hr. Hawaii	$25.75/hr. Hawaii
	$25.00/hr. Alaska	$30.00/hr. Alaska
Evenings, Weekends and Holidays	$ 7.75/hr.	$10.75/hr.
	$10.50/hr. Canada	$13.50/hr. Canada
	$12.75/hr. Hawaii	$15.75/hr. Hawaii
	$25.00/hr. Alaska	$28.00/hr. Alaska

CHAPTER 10
CompuServe

COMPUSERVE IS AN OUTGROWTH of an H&R Block subsidiary by the same name which began a remote data processing service in 1969. The remote service, based in Columbus, Ohio, offered telephone access to its main computers. For a fee, it handled payrolls, accounting, and storage services for companies that did not want to invest in their own mainframes.

The business clients, however, were using the Ohio mainframes only about 12 hours a day—the general business hours from coast to coast. On weekends and at night, the mainframes were sitting idle, although consuming expensive energy and manpower hours because they require 24-hour attention whether in use or not.

It wasn't and isn't an unusual problem. But in mid-1979, H&R Block implemented an innovative solution. They made their mainframes available to hobbyists and other individuals with programming expertise. Most "personal" computers of the era were home-assembled, either from kits or the local electronic parts store, and home computer enthusiasts were hungry for something to do beyond playing Pong games and drawing crude color pictures.

CompuServe called its system "MicroNET," and for a one-time, nine-dollar sign-on fee and five dollars an hour, pro-rated for each minute of use, the hobbyists could access the Ohio mainframes. They could do it only at night and on weekends, but that was all right, too. Most of them had regular jobs. The computers were what they played with when they came home.

It was a vast playground and the hobbyists used it well—writing programs, swapping programs, exploring possibilities and communicating with one another by CB-type chatter and by electronic mail. For many lonely hackers, it was like Robinson Crusoe discovering that there was a Friday on the island.

Growth was rapid. CompuServe quickly added stock quotes, news and weather information. A new industry was born.

Since then, CompuServe has retained much of its original flavor. A hobbyist-oriented utility, it is slower and less logically organized than Dow Jones or The Source. Hookup prices have risen to $19.95 but its other prices remain relatively the same. It can be accessed now 24 hours a day through its own CompuServe Network (numbers are listed in the Appendix) or through Telenet or the Canadian gateway, DATAPAC.

CompuServe isn't crisp enough for me. I want a utility that takes me directly to what I want without leading me through menus. But CompuServe's subscriber list, 56,000 and growing, indicates it has a lot of support. One reviewer compared it to an overstuffed bookstore, where you may have to browse a bit but you'll find some treasures.

We'll now take a sample tour of CompuServe.

There are a variety of terminals and personal computers which may be used to access CompuServe. Since different terminals have different features, each user should set his terminal type to get the most from the CompuServe service. After we sign on, we'll be asked to designate the terminal type. There will be four choices:

1 VIDTEX software compatible
2 ANSI compatible (VT-100)
3 Teleray
4 Other

VIDTEX compatible terminals are microcomputers running a program that emulates Videotex control codes.

VT-100 is a commercial unit. The control and escape codes used are compatible with ANSI (a form of computer code) standards.

Teleray 1061 is a commercial unit. The control and escape codes used are identical with VIDTEX.

Other is anything else, including my computer and most likely yours.

There are several ways to join CompuServe. The easiest and cheapest is through a Radio Shack store, which will sell a package containing a membership in both CompuServe and Dow Jones News Service for $20. Or, if you have an Apple or Radio Shack computer, you can buy the Radio Shack Videotex package, which will include the membership plus a disk containing a communications program. It is a bargain at $30.

You can also obtain packages through other computer stores. To obtain the names of those stores or to deal with CompuServe directly, phone customer service at 800-848-8990. You can write them at:

CompuServe Customer Service
PO Box 20212
Columbus, OH 43220

After joining and obtaining a password, we can sign on:

STEP ONE   Dial the local access number and wait for your communications software to inform you that you have established a connection.

STEP TWO   When the connection is made, hit **RETURN** or **ENTER** twice, then follow this sequence:

WHAT YOU SEE	WHAT YOU TYPE
User ID:	*(List the ID given by CompuServe.)*
Password:	*(List the password)*
CompuServe Information Service 19:17 EST Friday DD/MM/YY	
Choose one of the following:	
o Explanation of terminal types 1 VIDTEX software compatible 2 ANSI compatible (VT-100) 3 Teleray 4 Other	
Key choice	*4 (We choose number four.)*
Congratulations! Welcome to the exciting world of CompuServe Information Service. We are continually adding new services and we urge you to check "What's New" frequently.	
Don't be afraid of pressing the wrong keys. If you make a mistake you are given the chance to try again. Our Customer Service staff is ready to answer	

WHAT YOU SEE	WHAT YOU TYPE

any questions not provided in the CompuServe Information Service "User's Guide." Customer Service can be reached via FEEDBACK found under main menu item 5, or via the telephone numbers included in your package.

WHAT'S NEW

* New! The Computer Wire
* SKI Adds Resorts and Specials
* The Electronic Gourmet Debuts
* OAG EE Adds Nearest Airport
* EIS Subscription Kits Available
* Softex: Color Load 80 Programs

For details, see What's New Enter: GO NEW at the prompt on any page.

CompuServe   Page CIS-1

(The page reference CIS-1 is the title for the command menu.)

CompuServe Information Service

1 Home Services
2 Business & Financial
3 Personal Computing
4 Services for Professionals
5 User Information
6 Index

Enter your selection number, or H for more information

At this point, if you know a menu number, you can type a command to go directly to that menu. Otherwise, you may have to choose options from three or four menus to get where you want.

After practicing on CompuServe, you'll discover that you can by-pass menus by entering the command **"G-IND-99,"** which takes us to the menu page IND-99, which means page 99 of the index data base. This is the heart of the searching function of the CS index. We'll be prompted to enter a "keyword," a significant word in a title or text that describes the content of the text.

If we enter the word "shopping," for example, we'll see a list of the menus and page numbers relating to on-line shopping services. If we enter "finance," we will get a general list of finance-related menus.

A CompuServe
Special Interest Group

We then type the command for a specific finance menu: **G FIN-1**
The command takes us directly to the main menu of business and finance.
Of special interest is the command: **G HOM-5**
That takes us to the Groups and Clubs section of Home Services where
we will see a menu listing all the special interest groups on CompuServe.
These special interest sections are one of CompuServe's most popular features. There are more than 50 computerized clubs, each catering to people
with special interests, including cooking clubs where recipes are exchanged;
a golf club that lists specially priced tour packages and ticket offers to
major tournaments; and user clubs for most of the popular makes of
computers.

Special interest groups also are found with the command: **G SFP-1**.

This takes us to Services for Professionals, which has forums and information about various professions and special interest groups for doctors,
lawyers, educators, music lovers and writers.

Logging off CompuServe is quite easy. The command "Quit" usually will return you to a main prompt where an "Off" or a "Bye" will sign you off from the system.

Not only are CompuServe's data-base titles too numerous to explain in detail, but they change rapidly. The best way to find out what is available is by logging on and looking at CompuServe's index. We do this by waiting for CompuServe's main prompt (!), the exclamation point, and entering the command "G" or "GO," followed by the data-base name. Like this:

WHAT YOU SEE	WHAT YOU TYPE
CompuServe Page CIS-1	
CompuServe Information Service	
1 Home Services 2 Business & Financial 3 Personal Computing 4 Services for Professionals 5 User Information 6 Index	
Enter your selection number, or H for more information.	
	G IND (*We have asked CompuServe to take us directly to its index of data bases.*)
CompuServe Page IND-1	(*CompuServe displays its index data base, which begins with a list of options we can select.*)
INDEX 1 Search for Topics of Interest 2 List ALL Indexed Topics 3 Quick Index List 4 Explanation of Index	
	(*By giving us its exclamation point prompt, CompuServe is asking us to either select an option or give it another command*).

The first option, "Search for Topics of Interest," requests a topic you want to locate on the service. Enter the topic (i.e., stocks or news) followed by pressing the **ENTER** or **RETURN** key. You will then receive a menu showing a description and page number where the service is located.

The second option, "List ALL Index Topics," will display a complete list of all the indexed topics and their page numbers in alphabetic sequence. This index is quite long but may be used as the table of contents for the service. This option gives the page locations of available data bases. The page locations used with a GO command provide a quick access method as an alternative to passing through the menus.

The third option, "Quick Index List," provides the ability to list the index for a specific alphabetic character, such as the letter "C."

CompuServe offers more than 300 separate data bases. They range from programs on color graphics to money-market information to bank services to special newsletters for veterinarians, college professors and the like.

COMPUSERVE RATES

STANDARD CONNECT CHARGES—Available 6:00 P.M.–5:00 A.M., week-days, all day Saturday, Sunday and announced CompuServe holidays. (Time is determined by local time at location of network connection.)

$6.00/connect hour (300 Baud)

12.50/connect hour (1200 Baud)

Connect time is billed in one-minute increments, with a minimum of one minute per session.

PRIME CONNECT CHARGES—Available 8:00 A.M.–6:00 P.M., weekdays.

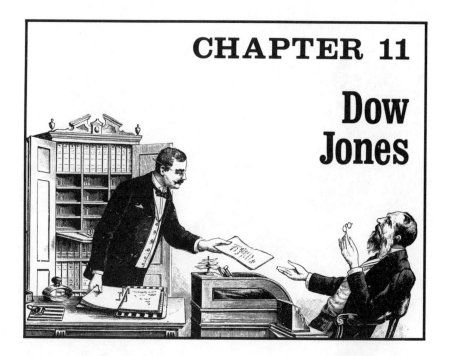

CHAPTER 11

Dow Jones

DOW JONES & COMPANY is probably the best-known distributor of financial information in the world. It was formed more than a century ago, in 1882, by three New York reporters: Charles Dow, Edward Jones and Charles Bergstresser. Yes, Bergstresser was a full partner. His name failed to become a household word because it was too long for the company letterhead. Really.

It was a straightforward operation with Jones editing stories written by Dow and Bergstresser. Clerks made multiple copies by handwriting one-page bulletins, which messengers delivered on foot and by bicycle to Wall Street subscribers.

The need for the information was so great that within seven years the one-page bulletin had expanded into the *Wall Street Journal.* At the beginning of the century, to further increase speedy delivery, the company created Dow Jones News Service, which used a teletype, called a "stock ticker," to carry breaking news and stock-price "quotations" into Wall Street offices and eventually the world.

By 1977 the ticker service had evolved into an electronic publishing service which was feeding information into time-sharing terminals, such as Telenet, and which was being accessed by dumb terminals in business offices. In the same year, Dow collaborated with a new computer company

The Many Careers of
Charles Bergstresser

called Apple to design a software package which allowed the Dow news to be received on microcomputers.

In 1980, a reorganization of Dow Jones created yet another branch of the tree—the Dow Jones News/Retrieval Service. It began business with a subscription list of 10,000 customers. By the end of 1983 the list had multiplied more than 10 times to more than 100,000 subscribers. Dow Jones claims it is the largest subscription base in the electronic publishing industry.

The service today is crisp and fast and fairly shines with quality.

At last count, it was offering 27 data bases, including stock market quotes, world and national news, financial news, sports, weather, movie reviews, electronic mail and an encyclopedia. There is something for everyone, but particularly for someone who invests in the stock market.

Telecommunications is particularly suited to the stock market. Indeed, it soon will be the stock market, or so predicts John Shad, chairman of the federal Securities Exchange Commission, which regulates the market.

Currently, investors can only monitor market information. To buy or sell stocks, they phone a broker.

By 1988, says Shad, investors will be able to enter their own market orders directly on their computer terminals and receive instant confirmations.

Such a development, he predicts, might eliminate stockbrokers as middlemen-clerks, and thus eliminate their commissions. Stockbrokers would instead spend more of their facilities on research and advice.

The key to the stock market, as with anything else in commerce, is to buy low and sell high. The people who consistently do that best are the people who have the most information. They pursue it with the ardor of racetrack junkies.

Another factor in the equation is not only to have better information than the other fellow but to have it sooner. Then you can buy the stock of a particular company lower because you know when something is about to happen to make it rise. On the other hand, if you see that a company is headed for a setback, you sell before the price of its stock falls.

This need to track performance and predict the future is what gave Dow Jones its start in the first place.

Membership in Dow Jones News/Retrieval is obtained through a variety of means, including direct contact with the company's 800 number (800-257-5114 as of this writing), or by buying Dow Jones software, or through packaging with other services, such as the $19.95 CompuServe package obtainable from Radio Shack.

Once you've joined, you call customer service to get a password and a local phone number. At that point, log-on procedures differ. Most likely, however, you'll communicate with Dow Jones via a local Telenet or Tymnet number.

The report includes 15-minute-delayed stock quotes and the latest news from the *Wall Street Journal, Barron's* and the Dow Jones News Service.

Other services include movie reviews, the *Academic American Encyclopedia,* Official Airline Guide, highlights of Merrill Lynch's investment research, a discount shopping service, news, sports and weather.

Dow Jones commands are preceded by two slashes, such as the command //**INTRO,** which calls up a newsletter for new users of the service. It provides a price list, hours of operation and some tips on how best to use the service.

After you have logged on, you will see:

MASTER MENU
* * *

A   Dow Jones Business and Economic News
B   Dow Jones Quotes
C   Financial And Investment Services
D   General News and Information Services
E   Mail Service and Free Customer Newsletter

Each of those choices represent a service "tier" of News/Retrieval. The services within those tiers are grouped according to price. (For a list of those prices, see the "Rates" box at the end of this chapter.)

To see the services listed under each of those categories, type the letter to the left and press **RETURN.** The services within each category are listed by their access symbol (the two slashes followed by a code of up to six letters).

A brief explanation of each data base is also included.

The Master Menu lists all of News/Retrieval's services, but you need not look at it before requesting a service. Once you are familiar with the data-base access symbols, you can enter any one of them immediately upon signing on to News/Retrieval by using the two-slash routine.

To log off Dow Jones, type **DISC** (for disconnect) anytime the screen stops scrolling and the cursor is in the left margin.

To sum up:

· Type two slashes (//) and the data-base code to access any data base in News/Retrieval.

· Type //**MENU** for a list of data bases.

· Type the word **HELP** after a data-base code to receive directions specific to that service.

· Type **DISC** (for disconnect) and press **RETURN** to sign off from Dow Jones News/Retrieval.

Current prices on stocks (delayed at least 15 minutes by the exchanges), options, bonds, mutual funds and other financial instruments are found in the Current Quotes service, //CQ.

To find the latest composite quote, type: //**CQ.** You will then receive a prompt asking you to enter stock symbol, such as **AAPL** for Apple Computer.

Example: **AAPL**

You can retrieve quotes on up to five stocks at a time by typing a space between the symbols.

Example: **ABC IBM CBS AAPL NBC**

If you don't know a stock symbol, type **//SYMBOL.** That is the on-line directory of symbols.

News on a particular company can be found as current as 90 seconds after the stories are sent over the Dow Jones News Service. Also, stories from the *Wall Street Journal* and *Barron's,* dating back 90 days, are available.

You can find the latest news about a company in several ways. The quickest is to use its stock symbol. For example, if you wish to find the latest news about Apple Computer, you would enter the following: **.AAPL 01**.

The dot or period (.) must precede the stock symbol. The symbol (AAPL) must be followed by a space and then by the numbers 01. The 01 is a code to display the latest headlines about the company.

Like this:

WHAT YOU SEE	WHAT YOU TYPE
ENTER QUERY	*.AAPL 01*
BG 01/27 APPLE COMPUTER WINS ROUND IN BATTLE AGAINST PIRATING	
BF 01/27 APPLE PINS MAC-INTOSH FUTURE ON TECHNI-CAL, MARKETING GAINS	
BE 01/24 APPLE INTRODUCES MACINTOSH AND THREE VERSIONS OF LISA	
BD 01/24 APPLE COMPUTER'S 1ST QUARTER NET PLUNGES 75% to 10C A SHARE	

You can then retrieve any story in the list by typing the two-letter access symbol to the left of each headline. The headline list is in a "last-in, first-out" format: the most recent news story is at the top of the list.

WHAT YOU SEE	WHAT YOU TYPE
	BE (We want to read the Jan. 24 story about the Apple Macintosh.)
01/24 APPLE INTRODUCES MACINTOSH (DW) AND THREE VERSIONS OF LISA CUPERTINO CALIF -DJ- AT ITS ANNUAL MEETING APPLE COMPUTER INC. INTRODUCED ITS LONG ANTICIPATED MACINTOSH COMPUTER AND THREE VERSIONS OF ITS TOP-OF-THE-LINE LISA COMPUTER. THE MACINTOSH WILL HAVE 128K OF MEMORY AND WILL SELL FOR $2,495. IT IS AVAILABLE IMMEDIATELY APPLE COMPUTER SAID. . . . (etc.)	

The data base also makes it possible to get industry, government or market news by using any of several codes developed for News/Retrieval.

For example, if you were interested in finding out how events in the broadcasting industry related to the American Broadcasting Company, you might look in the Telecommunications category.

Telecommunications is considered an "industry category," and its symbol is "TEL." To use it, enter the following: .I/TEL 01.

To access a Dow Jones data base, such as Dow Jones News, you must precede the command with two slashes. Once you have entered the data base, a period must precede any command. In this case, the "I/" before the symbol tells the computer you are interested in an industry category. Without it, Dow Jones News will treat "TEL" as a stock symbol.

Other Dow Jones data bases include //MEDGEN, which gives fundamental and market data on companies; //HQ, a data base of historical stock quotes; //EARN, which estimates company earnings; and // DSCLO, which provides wide-ranging company profiles based on information filed with the Securities and Exchange Commission.

In addition, News/Retrieval provides a wide array of general interest and other services.

Services such as //NEWS and //SPORTS use easy-to-follow menus as a guide.

Other services that use menus include weather (//WTHR), highlights of the *Wall Street Journal* (//WSJ), movie reviews (//MOVIES), the Forbes Directory (//FORBES), the Merrill Lynch Research Service (//MLYNCH) and the *Japan Economic Daily* (//KYODO).

DOW JONES RATES

Under the News/Retrieval pricing structure, the data bases are organized into five services, each with its own price.

Also, News/Retrieval is available under three plans: Standard Membership, Blue Chip Membership and Executive Membership. All rates are subject to change. In general, the rates are:

Prime Time Rate per Minute

Standard	Blue Chip	Executive
$1.20	$1.20	$.80

Non-Prime Time Rate per Minute

Standard	Blue Chip	Executive
$.20	$.13	$.13

Usage rates for customers accessing News/Retrieval directly are divided into prime and non-prime hours as follows:

Time Zone	Prime	Non-prime
Eastern	6:00 A.M.–6:00 P.M.	6:01 P.M.–4:00 A.M.
Central	5:00 A.M.–6:00 P.M.	6:01 P.M.–3:00 A.M.
Mountain	4:00 A.M.–6:00 P.M.	6:01 P.M.–2:00 A.M.
Pacific	3:00 A.M.–6:00 P.M.	6:01 P.M.–1:00 A.M.

NOTE: If you log on before 6:01 P.M. local time, the entire session will be billed as prime time.

CHAPTER 12

Delphi

IN 1982 AND 1983, several new services came on line offering information of use to the general public in the manner of The Source, Dow Jones and CompuServe. The newcomers included BRS After Dark, NewsNet and Delphi.

Delphi was the most rounded of these, offering the expected features of electronic mail, bulletin boards, news, shopping, and travel services. It obviously intends to compete for the same customers as The Source and CompuServe.

Delphi is operated out of Cambridge, Massachusetts, by the General Videotex Corporation. As a new service, its listings change and some of its better features are neither advertised nor found in the owner's manual.

Delphi began as an on-line encyclopedia in October 1981, founded by Wes Kussmaul, a Boston software and marketing consultant, who acquired "electronic publishing rights" of an encyclopedia owned by the Cadillac Publishing Company. Using optical scanning, a technology that converts a printed page to electrical signals, Kussmaul transferred the published contents of the existing encyclopedia to computer memory and added a significant amount of updated material.

Relying on the expertise found in the Massachusetts electronic community, Kussmaul soon expanded his encyclopedia service into a full general-information data base.

ALTERNATIVES

Several low-cost commercial data bases are directed at specific customer profiles, rather than the mass audience sought by The Source, Dow Jones, Delphi and CompuServe.

Foremost among the special-interest bases are Knowledge Index, BRS/After Dark and NewsNet.

Knowledge Index, 800-227-1927, is a subsidiary of Dialog and currently allows customers to use 21 of Dialog's most popular bases during nighttime hours and weekends. There is a sign-up fee of $35, and after that, on-line service costs $24 per hour, with no minimum charge and no extra charge. It offers abstracts and/or citations on virtually any subject you can think of. It doesn't offer full-text articles. Full text, however, usually can be ordered on line. It will be located and mailed to you by another company, Information On Demand (IOD), and costs about $4.50 per article plus 20 cents per page copying fee. If you want it fast, IOD can send the article to you by electronic mail for an additional fee. Knowledge Index by itself is one of the best research services, and bargains, in the industry. In tandem with IOD, it's unbeatable.

BRS/After Dark, 800-833-4707, is a conceptual clone of Knowledge Index. It is a subsidiary of the encyclopedic data base BRS and offers non-business-hour use of 28 of BRS's data bases, most of them different from those of Knowledge Index. It is like having a university library on line at your office or home. In some bases it carries abstracts and in others full text. There is a sign-up fee of $50 and a monthly minimum charge of $12. On-line fees range from $6 to $20, depending on which bases you use. If it weren't for the monthly minimum, I'd recommend this service. On the other hand, if you do a lot of academic research and know you'll be on line at least two hours a month, this could be your cup of tea.

NewsNet, 800-345-1301, offers electronic versions of more than 100 newsletters. Subjects range from communications and computers to government regulations and investment. The service contains three basic bases: NewsNet, which carries current newsletters; NewFlash, a clipping service providing information on topics of your choice; and Library, which carries back issues. NewsNet is on line all day every day and costs about $24 per hour of use. There is no sign-up fee, but there is a monthly minimum of $15. NewsNet offers an incredible range of experts who are feeding information that is sometimes only hours old. For investors, journalists and anyone who needs to know about the leading edge of trends, NewsNet is a must. For others, it's probably a waste of money.

The result is Delphi, which opened its services to the public in February 1983.

Its basic services are reasonably priced, with a one-time sign-on charge of $50 and nighttime and weekend on-line fees of only five dollars. A very nice additional feature is that several people can use a single membership. Although this feature is common in industrial data bases, such as Dialog, it isn't duplicated (to my knowledge) in the general purpose services.

Delphi can be joined by contacting Delphi directly at:

DELPHI
General Videotex Corporation
3 Blackstone St.
Cambridge, MA 02139
617-491-3393

Delphi has no minimum monthly charge. Its sole pricing handicap, however, is a big one. Delphi charges extra for computer shopping, news and an airlines guide. The extra charges are much higher than dealing through the big three or by dealing directly with the shopping or airlines data bases. The high rates probably are designed to compensate for the lower rates charged to all-purpose users. The high surcharges are a definite handicap, and I question the wisdom of Delphi's marketing strategy on this point.

At this writing, Delphi is slower than The Source or Dow Jones, although comparable to CompuServe in speed. Being slower means more on-line time and more time on the meter. As long as you're dealing with bulletin boards and the non-surcharge items, Delphi's lower costs still tend to make it cheaper than the others. But once you get into serious information gathering, the price skyrockets.

Delphi, however, has recognized its slowness and promises that its speed eventually will surpass its competitors.

To build a subscription base, Delphi in early 1984 began offering a $69.95 package deal which included a lifetime subscription to Delphi, a $20 user's handbook, two free hours of service and a free Volksmodem. The latter itself costs $69 at retail list.

On screen, Delphi is the friendliest of the general services I've encountered. But I find it best suited for browsing and would use it only as a supplementary service.

To illustrate its friendliness, however, let me introduce you to the system.

STEP ONE   Dial the local access number and wait for your communications software to inform you that you have established a connection.

STEP TWO   When the connection is made, hit **RETURN** or **ENTER** twice, then follow this sequence:

WHAT YOU SEE	WHAT YOU TYPE
TYMNET	
TERMINAL=	*A*
PLEASE LOG ON:	*Delphi*
DELPHI CONNECTED	
Username:	*CLARK*
Password	*GABLE*
Logon at: DD/MM/YY 19:10:45	
Last Logon: DD/MM/YY 08:12:53	

Hello CLARK

Welcome to Delphi V1.7
Copyright (c) 1983
General Videotex Corporation

You may add additional members to your account at any time by sending mail to SERVICE and requesting the membernames.

MAIN Menu:

APPOINTMENT-CALENDAR
BULLETIN-BOARDS
CONFERENCE
DELPHI-ORACLE
EXIT
FINANCIAL-SERVICES
GAMES
GUIDED TOUR
HELP
INFOMANIA
LIBRARY
MAIL

BULLETIN-BOARDS gives you access to the on-line bulletin boards. Bulletin boards exist for a variety of categories and topics. In the above example, when Delphi asks what you want to do, you reply, "Bulletin Boards." Delphi will come back and ask, "Which Bulletin Board?" At that point, type a question mark and you will see a list of the available BB's. Following some BB names will be a status symbol. (P) stands for Private and (R) stands for Read only.

Bulletin boards on Delphi include:

APPLE	*MOVIES*
ATARI	*NEWTON APPLE KIDS*
BOOKS	*ORACLE*
CHATTER	*PERFORMING ARTISTS NETWORK*
COMPUTERS	*PERSONALS*
CPM	*PRINTERS,MODEMS,ETC*
DECUS (R)	*RACING*
DELPHI (R)	*SOFTWARE*
DIGITAL	*SPACE RESEARCH*
GAMES	*SPORTS*
HAM RADIO	*TRAVEL*
IBM-PC	*TRIVIA*
JOKES	*TRS80*
MARINE RESEARCH	*USER ADVISORY PANEL*
MISCELLANY	*VIC-COMMODORE*

Apart from the bulletin boards, Delphi has a number of innovative services which include the following:

APPOINTMENT-CALENDAR   allows you to record all your appointments by day, time and person. You can also obtain a list of such appointments with a specific person, at a specific time, or on a specific date.

DELPHI-ORACLE   gives you access to an on-line battery of experts in a wide variety of topics. By using this system you can submit your questions on any number of topics, including: using the DELPHI system; computer-related topics; and sources for information. Your questions will be routed to the appropriate resident expert, who will respond within a short period of time.

FINANCIAL-SERVICES   In financial services, you can pay your bills through BANKING, receive help in managing your home finances through the programs in the HOME program Library, attend to business needs in the BUSINESS Program Library, receive valuable investment advice from Security Objective Services (ADVISORY SERVICES), or actually establish and maintain a relationship with North American Investment Corporation under BROKERAGE SERVICES.

GAMES   are separated by category, according to the type of game, be it board game, sports game or adventure. As some of these games use types of commands that are different from the rest of the Delphi system, you should read the HELP on the games before playing them. The HELP files include a description of the game, how the game is played, and, sometimes, strategy hints. If you have specific questions regarding the games, either post a message in the GAMES bulletin board, in the SIGS category, or submit a question to ORACLE.

INFOMANIA is where members share their talent, knowledge and literary creativity with other members in a wide variety of ways. Members may read the contributed works of their peers in NEWSLETTERS and AUTHORS, run programs in the member program library, MEMBERS' CHOICE, take polls of other members' opinions on any topic, or add chapters to one of the DELPHI COLLABORATIVE NOVELS.

POLL allows you to create a poll, list available polls, vote and see the results of a particular poll. The polls created will remain active (can be voted on) for one month; after this period, the poll will become inactive and will remain in that state for two weeks. During those two weeks you can only see the result of the poll. The poll will be deleted after two weeks.

LIBRARY gives you access to a variety of library services, such as the Kussmaul encyclopedia, Dialog Research Library and ITT/Dialcom Information Service. Also, the Delphi-Info section is here and contains valuable hints on using these services as well as general information, such as data access numbers and information on ordering manuals.

LIBRARIAN is the off-line research service of Delphi. Here you can ask researchers to investigate for you. Any topic can be chosen and questions can be researched to any depth. The current charge for the research is $25 an hour, plus a fee for delivering the document either on line or by mail. A detailed quotation will be sent within two days of a request.

ON-LINE MARKETS is divided into four selections:
1) BAZAAR enables DELPHI members to post items for sale or bid, and allows other members to respond to the items.
2) CATALOG connects you with DELPHI's on-line companies. It allows you to list or browse through data by product or company. You may also search data on any combination of the product, company and category. After finding the items you want, you can order them direct from the company by credit card or C.O.D. For information about posting your ad on DELPHI, send a MAIL message to SERVICE.
3) COMP-U-STORE is a gateway through DELPHI into an on-line shopping center. It allows comparison shopping for more than 35,000 items without leaving the house. When you find the item you desire you may place an order for it on line, at a substantial saving.

4) SPECIALTY-SERVICES takes you to a sub-menu that contains a variety of special items and services offered by members of DELPHI.

TRAVEL enters you into the interactive travel system. Once in this system you can access information on transportation schedules, plan your travel itinerary and order actual tickets on line. The travel services are offered to you by Delphi and Fresh Pond Travel, Inc., of Cambridge, Massachusetts. The travel services are a sign-up service; you must be signed up in advance to use this command. The service is free. DELPHI will provide information on signing up for this service. The first time you use the travel system you will be asked to create a preference form so that any future requests you can make can be handled in the most expeditious manner. You can create either a personal preference form (for your personal travel) or a corporate form (for business use). In either case, the information is kept confidential.

TRAVEL INFORMATION enters you into the information subsystem. In this system you can obtain information in six different areas: information on cruises, charter flights, scheduled airline service, hotels, vacation packages and car rentals. Each menu item displays a questionnaire; in most cases the information sought is evident from the prompt. Requests for information are not binding in any way on you. The response will come back to you in a short time via DELPHI's electronic mail.

DELPHI RATES

MEMBERSHIP FEE: $49.95
BASIC CONNECT TIME: $6.00 per hour, weekends, holidays and after 6:00 P.M. Daytime, 5:00 A.M.–6:00 P.M., $16.00 per hour.
  There is no extra charge for using 1,200-Baud modem.

CHAPTER 13
Videotex

IN THIS CHAPTER we're going to look at something that is a terrific idea struggling to survive. I speak of "videotex." "Videotex" refers to the receipt of information services in the home, usually with the home TV used as a display monitor. Delivered by phone, broadcast waves or cable, the videotex comes into the house as signals that must be decoded and displayed. This is done by an unscrambling device supplied by the videotex service.

Broadly speaking, the major information services, such as The Source or Dow Jones, are videotex because they exchange data using a video display. More specifically, however, videotex has come to mean local services such as those operated by Times-Mirror in the Los Angeles area, Keycom in Chicago and Viewtron in southern Florida. Although England's videotex system, called Prestel, is a national system, its focal point is local—namely, London.

Unlike the text-oriented displays of Dow Jones et al., videotex uses lots of color graphics. It comes on the screen in pages, like a full-color magazine.

Videotex is mainly a marriage between an information vendor and a dumb terminal. The display monitor for the dumb terminal is the TV set.

Slowly—and hopefully—in the years to come we'll be hearing more

TWO WAYS OF
LOOKING AT THINGS

Videotex, basically, is an information system brought into the home through a telephone connection or a special cable-TV hookup.

A videotex customer replies to the television (or monitor) screen's questions by punching commands back through the system on an electronic keyboard. This is what allows the customer to order merchandise, make bank transfers and conduct other business.

A close cousin to videotex, and a probable competitor for customers and advertising, is teletext, a one-way signal beamed over television airwaves to special receivers or sent through cable-TV hookups. The display is seen on the television screen and is selected as one would select any other TV channel.

Teletext customers can pick and choose from a menu of information similar to that provided by videotex, although generally much smaller because of the limitations of a TV signal. But customers can't "talk back" to teletext. They can't order fruit baskets, for example, or make plane reservations. They can, however, look at the air schedules.

about videotex. I say "hopefully" because the system is struggling to be born and has many handicaps. Both American and foreign videotex systems have only a small number of subscribers and are limited in the quantity and quality of the data bases offered. Compounding those deficiencies is the cost—an average minimum fee of $40 per month.

If videotex can get its costs down, it may become the standard medium for all popular data-base communications. First of all, it is easy to use. Touch one button and the TV set switches to videotex. Touch another button and you have your banking information. Or a local department store's catalog. Or the high school sports scores. With videotex there is no need to concern yourself with modems, communications software or what type of computer to buy. It is all there in a single package.

Videotex's second big advantage is that it is home-oriented, like the local newspaper. The videotex system you watch in Miami, Florida, will not be the videotex you watch in Los Angeles. Like the newspaper, it will have local, national and international data bases. There will be local advertising, local news, local sports, local banking, local shopping, local want ads. At the same time there will be access to national and international information. But the emphasis is local. You do not find local on Dow Jones.

The industry is currently in the early stages of development and one indication of this is the lack of standardization.

There are four basic videotex systems operating in various parts of the world and all are incompatible with one another. The first of these is Prestel, developed by British Telecom and introduced in 1979. Prestel has about 25,000 subscribers, most of whom are interested in business information. But it carries a number of consumer-oriented features, including restaurant and travel information. The Prestel system of graphics communication is used in Great Britain, Germany, Italy, Austria, Belgium, Norway and the Netherlands as a basis for their own videotex systems.

A better system in terms of graphics is Canada's Telidon, which provides pictures and designs more pleasing to consumers and advertisers. An even higher-resolution system is used in Japan.

In 1981, AT&T used Canada's Telidon as the basis for a new American system called North American Presentation Level Protocol Syntax (NAPLPS). That system is the one in most common use in experiments in the United States. Canada and France are modifying their systems to be compatible.

The first commercial U.S. system to come on line was South Florida's Viewtron, operating out of Miami and targeted at the affluent communities in Dade, Broward and Palm Beach counties. Aimed at households aged 25 to 49 with a minimum $35,000 income, it began service in October 1983. Initially Viewtron officials expected to sign up 5,000 households the first year, but later lowered the goal to 2,000.

The system is simple to acquire. You rent a terminal and decoder box from Viewtron for $40 a month, which includes ten hours of user time. The terminal keyboard is cordless and sends its signals to the decoder box via infrared pulses—like using a remote tuner on your TV. The box has two wires in the back; one plugs into the TV set and the other into a telephone modular jack. Being wireless, the keyboard can be operated from anywhere in the room.

What I'm saying here, and a big part of the appeal, is that you can lie on the couch and drink beer or eat bonbons while you do whatever you want to do with Viewtron.

Viewtron offers more than 300 categories of information and services, including breaking news, which we get faster than we would in the newspapers or broadcast media. This news includes quite a bit of local news, right down to neighborhoods. You can also access national and international news, including news related to specific areas, such as Latin America, or Asia and the Pacific.

You can read the New York *Times,* bank at home, shop at home; look at sports, restaurants and stock market reports; watch weather conditions; read the encyclopedia; get airline schedules; peruse local advertising and check the electronic mail.

There are movie reviews, television listings and a calendar of things going on in the region. You can review bulletin boards, gardening hints and household tips, and query a sex counselor. If inclined toward self-improvement, you can take language courses or a variety of other educational programs.

You can even turn it on before leaving for work and check the traffic situation. On Miami's Viewtron, traffic reports are updated every 10 minutes during morning rush hours.

In sum, Viewtron offers many of the features of the major data bases plus all the local material. However, the videotex-only terminals can't store or edit the information. Nor can they transmit or print long files.

Already, the landscape is littered with huge American corporations which thought they could make videotex work.

Two of these, NBC and CBS, recently abandoned years-long experiments with a one-way version of videotex called "teletext."

I say "one-way" because in normal videotex you can instruct your terminal to do limited chores, such as banking or making ticket reservations. On teletext we just wait for whatever happens on the TV screen.

Teletext bypasses the costly phone system and comes at the viewer over the airwaves. Your interaction is restricted to choosing what you want to look at. Network teletext transmits information on the upper edge of the TV screen. If you look closely at a network program, you can see a small black band at the top. This band carries 21 lines of unused transmission space. One of the bands is used for captioned broadcasts to the hard-of-hearing. Experimental teletext uses five bands which are invisible except to a decoder box.

Teletext solves the cost factor. The decoder boxes are no more expensive than those used on cable systems.

But it lacks the two main selling points of videotex: local orientation and interaction.

The future may see a marriage of the two systems.

Keycom, a joint venture of Centel, Field Enterprises and Honeywell, is delving into both videotex and teletext. Time Inc. and NBC have chosen instead to develop information for teletext services. Two studies by consulting firms have offered hope for a fairly strong public response to videotex.

Booz, Allen and Hamilton Inc. predicts that videotex will be in 5 to 10 percent of U.S. households by 1990. CSP International claims videotex and teletext together will be in 17 percent of those households by then, with videotex getting slightly more than half that market.

But concrete results will have to back up those predictions before anyone makes money. Viewtron, by pitching to upper-income families, hopes to be present in 18 cities by 1985.

Another system, the Times-Mirror "Gateway" service in southern California, plans to be in 13 cities by 1986.

A Keycom exec says that watching the industry set out to meet those expectations reminds him of the turn-of-the-century days when would-be airplane inventors hitched up their wings and bounded off the nearest cliff. "A lot of people crashed before the Wright Brothers came along," he adds.

A combination of teletext's cheap delivery system and videotex's local services already is in the works. In February 1984 three blue-chip companies—IBM, CBS and Sears Roebuck—announced they were joining forces to offer videotex to owners of personal computers.

The new service isn't scheduled to start until at least 1985. But it would allow personal computer owners to shop, bank and receive information at home while dealing with local companies.

Subscribers would shop at home for merchandise from the Sears catalog, insurance from Allstate, financial services from Dean Witter Reynolds and real estate from Coldwell Banker. "Merchandise from competing manufacturers" also would be offered, according to a Sears spokesman.

Indications were that CBS wants to set up local and regional operations initially and then connect the systems into a national network.

Right now, videotex is caught in a marketing dilemma. In order for the service to be profitable in both on-line fees and advertising revenue, it must attract a mass market. In order to attract a mass market it must be cheaper. But it can't be cheaper until it has a mass market.

Or can it? Whoever solves the dilemma can make a fortune and do a public service at the same time.

CHAPTER 14

The High-Tech Connections

THIS CHAPTER might more appropriately be entitled "High-Priced Data Bases" because unless you know what you are doing, these utilities can empty the bank account fast.

I still get nervous when I sign on to one.

The services to be discussed in this chapter are primarily used by professional researchers. Used properly, they are well worth the money and, in fact, usually prove cheaper than conventional research techniques. The services contain, by industry estimate, more than 80 percent of all information published in the past 15 years—in the world.

You can, for example, search each of the 4,800 yellow-pages directories published in the United States, looking for any combination of names, occupations, professions and locations you choose. The searches can be performed in a matter of minutes, sometimes seconds.

Using the services is both a skill and an art. In most instances, it takes

---

THIMK

Don't go on line with these data bases until you have consulted the manuals and planned your search commands in advance.

at least two days of classroom instruction plus 15 to 20 hours of practice to learn the proper commands of an information service such as Dialog. The command techniques, however, are merely the tools of the trade. The artistic part comes in a feel for the subject, the Sherlock Holmes–like ability to go to the heart of the hunt.

An example of a high-tech researcher is Maureen Corcoran of Gainesville, Florida. Blond, photogenic, in her late twenties, she operates a two-person research firm called the American Information Corporation. Using two micros, hard-disk storage, a Hayes Smartmodem, two printers and a small collection of reference books, she produces reports; locates experts; tracks industry trends; provides background on specific persons, companies or topics and provides support material for business marketing.

Her clients are ad agencies, businesses that want investment information, law offices and political groups. They pay from $300 to $1,500 per report. They include:

• A food industry conglomerate which wanted to start a gourmet foods company but first asked Corcoran to put together a world-wide directory of sources for caviar, quality cheeses and other gourmet foods.

• An attorney whose client had incurred lung damage when he accidentally burned the insulation on a piece of kitchen equipment. The lawyer wanted Corcoran to find if inhaling fumes from polyurethane-based insulation could cause permanent lung damage.

• Another attorney who wanted to know if there was "something wrong with the bumpers on 1976 Volkswagens."

To get the answers, she relies on such data bases as Dialog and Bibliographic Retrieval Service.

When we talk about these data bases we are talking major leagues. They are the heavy hitters of the information services, the ones that provide virtually everything you want to know about anything you ever heard of. Here's the lineup:

DIALOG   3460 Hillview Ave., Palo Alto, CA 800-227-1927. This is a division of the Lockheed Corporation which builds aircraft and missiles. Originally developed for internal use at Lockheed, Dialog went public in 1972 and now counts nearly half a million subscribers in more than 50 nations. It offers more than 200 data bases containing more than 80 million records. Dialog doesn't charge for signing up and has no monthly minimum. You pay only for what you use. One thing you will need is the Dialog manual which tells you how to use it. That costs $40. The average Dialog search costs about $90 an hour.

BRS (BIBLIOGRAPHIC RETRIEVAL SERVICE) 1200 Route 7, Latham, NY, 12110. 800-833-4707. BRS went on line in 1976 and was aimed primarily at medical center libraries and other technical information centers. It is now a well-rounded, academically oriented data base with millions of records pertaining to business, financial, medical, scientific and educational subjects. BRS's sign-up costs are so varied as to be confusing. Basically, you pay $50 as down payment against future services. BRS is less extensive than Dialog but also less expensive.

MEAD DATA CENTRAL PO Box 933, Dayton, OH 45401. 800-227-4908. This is the vendor of LEXIS, a vast law library, and NEXIS, a full-text library of stories in more than 60 American and foreign periodicals. It also includes a full-text patent searching base. It offers full-text retrieval from the New York *Times,* United Press International, Associated Press, Reuters, and Chinese and Japanese news services. The Mead services are expensive, and the price structure was being revised at the time of this writing.

SDC/ORBIT 2500 Colorado Avenue, Santa Monica, CA 90406. 800-421-7229. SDC (Systems Development Corporation) created the first modern on-line retrieval system when it came on line in 1965. In 1974 it twinned itself, making SDC the search service aspect of the company and creating ORBIT as the on-line library. It has nearly 100 data bases of more than 55 million records divided into 13 information categories: Business, Chemistry, Engineering, Electronics, Energy, Environment, Government, Industry-Specific, Life Science, Multidisciplinary Studies, Patents, Social Science, and Science and Technology. ORBIT's special appeal is that it has data bases others don't have. For instance, the data base COLD has information from all sciences dealing with Antarctica. In terms of finding information, ORBIT may be the heaviest hitter of all. But it is difficult to learn and as a consequence is costly to join. There is no sign-up fee, but an absolutely necessary training package costs $125. Its on-line costs are about the same as Dialog's.

I.P. SHARP Box 418, Exchange Tower, 2 First Canadian Place, Toronto, Ontario M5X 1E3, Canada. 416-364-5361. I have never been on this data base but I have a friend, a professional researcher, who is terrified of it. He says he ran up a $90 bill once and was on line less than 10 minutes. This Canadian firm provides more than 90 data bases relating to aviation, economics, energy, finances, insurance and banking. It provides vast amounts of raw statistical data that can be used to create models of business or sociological situations. It requires no sign-up fee and its on-line time-sharing costs seem low at $1 per hour. However, they charge 70 cents for every thousand characters you send or receive from their computer and 45 cents per "computer processor unit" you occupy, whatever that means. It can be accessed through Tymnet or Telenet in the United States.

The most typical and in many ways the most formidable of the above services is Dialog. It can provide instant access to such data bases as:

Medline—Dating from 1966, it has more than four million records updated monthly by the U.S. National Library of Medicine in Bethesda, Maryland. It is one of the major sources in the world for biological and medical literature.

ORDINARY ENGLISH

In the 1957 movie *Desk Set,* Spencer Tracy runs a Univac-like computer which makes up payrolls, answers esoteric research questions and drives librarians Katharine Hepburn and Joan Blondell to distraction. Ever since that movie, or maybe before then, the popular idea has been that you communicate with computers by typing messages to them in plain English, such as "What was Lou Gehrig's lifetime slugging average?" or "List our top five salesmen in the Midwest."

Unfortunately, that's not the way it is done.

To go after Lou Gehrig on Dialog's mainframe computer, we'd first have to order it to **BEGIN** a data base and then **SELECT** all files containing the words **LOU** and **GEHRIG** and **BASEBALL** and **LIFETIME** and **SLUGGING AVERAGE.**

We have to go through the same rigamarole on any data base on any subject. Computers don't normally respond to plain English.

But that may change. A lot of work is being done on "artificial intelligence," a branch of computer science that teaches machines to simulate human thought. Among the early results of the work are software programs that allow users to ask computers questions in ordinary English.

Three such programs were demonstrated at a three-day software convention in New Orleans in February 1984. Two of the programs, exhibited by Microrim Corporation of Bellevue, Washington, and Artificial Intelligence of Waltham, Massachusetts, allow people to search for information in large mainframes by posing questions in ordinary English. A third program, called In-Search and manufactured by the Menlo Corporation in San Jose, California, allows callers to reduce Dialog's intricate command procedures to a few simple words.

Magazine Index—Dating from 1959, it is the first on-line data base to offer truly broad coverage of general interest magazines. It covers nearly 400 popular magazines and provides extensive coverage of current affairs, the performing arts, business, sports, recreation and travel, consumer product evaluations, science and technology and other areas.

D&B Million Dollar Directory—Comprises information on more than 120,000 companies which have a net worth of more than $500,000, and includes hard-to-find information on businesses that are privately held, as well as publicly owned companies. Its list includes annual sales, number of employees and the names of top officers.

Trade Opportunities—Dating from 1976, it provides leads to export opportunities for U.S. businesses. The information is supplied by U.S. State Department foreign service officers who describe products of interest from foreign governments or companies.

Electronic Yellow Pages—Contains names, addresses, phone numbers and other information on more than nine million individuals and companies. That's right. *Nine million.* The yellow pages are divided into seven separate "directories."

The Construction Directory provides information on contractors, construction agencies, housing contractors, industrial builders, highway construction companies, steel and concrete work contractors, as well as plumbing, masonry, painting and heating service contractors.

The Financial Services Directory lists banks, savings and loan institutions and credit unions in the United States.

The Manufacturers Directory lists half a million U.S. manufacturers in all types of industry.

The Professionals Directory lists professionals in insurance, real estate, medicine, law, engineering and accounting.

The Retailers Directory lists nearly three million retail establishments, including lumber stores, paint stores, gasoline stations, clothing stores, bars, restaurants and florists.

The Services Directory contains another two million listings of companies engaged in business, financial, office and recreational services. These include hotels and motels.

The Wholesalers Directory lists one million wholesale dealers in all types of goods.

Dialog is as easy to access as The Source, CompuServe or any of the other information services. In fact, it is dialed up using the same equipment and software and routes through Uninet, Telenet or Tymnet.

Because the data bases are expensive, ranging from $25 to more than

$100 an hour, it is highly advised to plan searches in advance. The costs are prorated to the closest minute and a well-planned search can be done for less than fifty dollars.

An adjunct of Dialog is Knowledge Index, a $24-an-hour nighttime and weekend service which provides quick and low-cost summaries of more than 14 million articles, reports and books. These summaries, or listings, are called "abstracts." They include such data bases as the U.S. National Agricultural Library; all books in print; physics, electronics, power systems and utilities; the International Software Data Base; Standard & Poor's News; the Educational Resources Information Center; Engineering Literature; Government Printing Office Reference Files; the National Technical Information Service; the Magazine Index of stories which have appeared in American magazines since 1959; Medline coverage of medicine, dentistry, nursing and health care; International Pharmaceutical Abstracts; and the National Newspaper Index, which provides a front-to-back indexing of newspapers, including the New York *Times* and the *Wall Street Journal.*

Dialog, BRS and the other high-tech services also deliver really esoteric information, such as the *Alcohol Information Retrieval System,* which covers scientific and technical international studies on alcohol and alcohol problems. Then there is *Adtrack,* indexing all advertisements of one-quarter page or larger appearing in 148 major consumer magazines; *Foundations Grants Index; Chemical Regulations and Guidelines System; Weldasearch* and *Social Scisearch.*

Another information service, WESTLAW, provides access to an entire law library. It will allow clients to read the full text of such legal libraries as Federal Statutory Law; Federal Regulations; Federal Case Law; Federal Special Interest Libraries; Attorney General Opinions; and Black's Law Dictionary.

In other systems there is the ORR System of Construction Costs data base. For the shipping industry there is Maritime Data Network. And for students there is, among others, the *Encyclopaedia Britannica* with the full text of *Britannica 3* and the 10-volume *Micropaedia,* which contains encyclopedia information in capsule form.

The services I've outlined above are for use by anyone, but they are intended for professionals. Dialog, BRS, Westlaw and the others are renting the use of their powerful mainframes and costs quickly mount. The costs include not only the sign-up and on-line fees but also the manuals, which are absolutely necessary. It also is useful, and profitable, for users to attend the regular seminars given in major cities by the various information services.

The total costs are affordable by middle-sized to large corporations or even by some small companies like Maureen Corcoran's research service in Gainesville, Florida. But they are far too expensive for casual browsing.

Meanwhile, a new and less expensive series of data bases is now being formed. For the first time, the general public will be using computers to tap one of America's greatest information sources.

CHAPTER 15

Newspaper Libraries

NEWSPAPER LIBRARIES are one of the world's true treasures. The early libraries of newspapers were simply the collection of back issues. If an issue sold out, the library was that much poorer.

Newspaper indexes began to appear in the early 1700s, the first being the Maryland *Gazette* (1727–1746). The Hartford *Courant* began indexing in its first year of publication, 1764. Canada's first newspaper index was begun by the *Royal American Gazette* in 1787.

Those papers, however, were isolated phenomena. It was the approaching Civil War that caused newspapers in America to build libraries and indexes. Both the New York *Tribune* and the New York *Herald* began libraries and indexes in 1860, followed by the New York *Times* in 1861.

About the same time the New York *Times* began indexing back issues, it and other newspapers began preparing advance obituaries. Biographies of prominent and usually elderly people were written in advance and set in type. When the person died, the presses would stop, the newsroom would write one or two paragraphs reporting the death and then the pre-set type would be added. It could be done in minutes, and in those days of 12 editions a day and more than 20 dailies in New York City, woe to the paper which didn't have its "morgue" of pre-set obituaries. The morgue, already a library and storage room for pre-set type, became the natural storehouse for clipped stories.

A century later, in the 1960s, newspapers entered the electronic age when many converted to photo-electrical equipment to set type and print papers. As computers came more and more into use, they were used to write stories and set type, and thus an electronic library of all stories written was created. At first, such libraries were used only by newsroom personnel. But from the beginning it was realized that there was good marketing potential for selling the information to the general public.

In 1969 the New York *Times* began marketing computerized information services through its newly created Information Bank. This experiment was nobly supported by the *Times* through the 1970s. By 1980 the service had two million story subjects on file and had acquired citations and story summaries from 90 other publications as diverse as the Atlanta *Constitution* and the Japan *Economical Journal,* the Washington *Post* and the *Bulletin of Atomic Scientists.*

The service was limited, however, in that it gave only one- to three-paragraph summaries of entire stories. The Information Bank might give you a citation and summary for a Coca-Cola article in the Atlanta *Constitution,* but not the full text of the story.

The step to "full text" marketing of stories came on June 1, 1980, when a new data base, The New York *Times*–On-Line, went on the market. This offered complete articles from the newspaper within 48 hours of publication.

Even though the service was expensive, costing more than $150 per hour of use, the *Times* couldn't make a profit off the system. In early 1983 the *Times* kept the system but sold the marketing of it to Mead Data Corporation, a New York communications company which was already marketing full-text stories of the Washington *Post* and 40 other newspapers, magazines and newsletters.

Mead Data, through its information service Nexis, offers extraordinary on-line information. For example, when Pope John Paul II was shot, the name of his attempted assassin, Mehmet Ali Agca, at first meant nothing to American TV network news staffs. However, a Nexis search revealed that Agca not only was an escaped murderer but also had written a letter in 1979 threatening to kill the Pope when the pontiff was in Turkey.

The business applications of such a service are dazzling. A lawyer can research the background of corporations, or search files for a new product name to see if anyone has used it. An advertising executive can check the background of a prospective client. A defense contractor can obtain knowledge of competitors in faraway cities.

Nexis, while less expensive than the old New York *Times* services, nevertheless has an average cost of more than $100 per hour. It also delivers only large publications—the *Times* and *Post, Newsweek,* the *Economist.*

If you're an Oklahoma City contractor and you want information about a Lexington, Kentucky, coal mine, you're not likely to get it from Nexis unless there was an article on it in those major publications.

But newspaper libraries are now on-line that will report on Oklahoma City and Lexington, Kentucky. And while they are expensive they are cheaper than Nexis. Furthermore, at whatever the cost, they are the forerunners of systems which will offer access to the libraries of newspapers nationwide, from large to small.

Traditionally, the world of electronic newspaper data bases has been reserved for those few like the *Times* and *Post* that are big enough to either go it alone or be invited aboard one of the general data bases, such as Nexis or Dow Jones.

But in 1982, Knight-Ridder Newspapers, Inc., owners of 35 newspapers from coast to coast and border to border, began marketing the libraries of the Philadelphia *Daily News* and the Philadelphia *Inquirer,* the latter being one of the best newspapers in the world in local, national and international coverage.

In terms of newspaper data bases or people who subscribe to them, "We'll take anybody and everybody," says Peter Leach, director of the Knight-Ridder service, which is called Vu/Text.

At the newspaper end, says Vu/Text marketing manager Donna Willmann, any newspaper with an electronic newsroom can link up with Vu/Text and offer its services on line.

At the subscriber end, virtually anyone with a micro and a modem can access the data base.

Newspapers are rapidly joining Vu/Text. By the fall of 1984, Vu/Text could offer full-text stories from both Philadelphia newspapers; the Washington *Post;* the Lexington, Kentucky, *Herald-Leader;* the Gary, Indiana, *Post-Tribune;* the (national) *Journal of Commerce;* the San Jose, California, *Mercury-News;* the Wichita, Kansas, *Eagle-Beacon,* the Associated Press and all seven newspapers of the Chicago *Tribune*/New York *Daily News* chain; the *Wall Street Transcript,* a weekly publication covering verbatim reports of round-table discussions by security analysts on various industries; interviews with executives on corporate product and service plans, and announcements and speeches; plus 80 data bases of QL Systems Limited, a Canadian information service which offers the complete Canadian Press News Wire, and a thorough array of Canadian legal and legislative libraries; the Miami *Herald;* the Detroit *Free Press;* PR Newswire, a service that carries press releases from over 8,000 sources, including a majority of all companies listed on national stock exchanges, government agencies, labor unions, nonprofit organizations, and virtually every major public relations agency.

Prices average about $60 per hour on line but range from $30 for use of the *Academic American Encyclopedia* to $295 for the blue-ribbon *Wall Street Transcript.*

While those prices seem similar to those of Nexis, they in fact are much cheaper. Nexis charges extra for a variety of items which Vu/Text delivers standard. And an independent bench-mark comparison by Seybold Publications indicated that Vu/Text is five times faster than Nexis. A typical search on Vu/Text which took twenty-five seconds took two minutes and five seconds on Nexis.

Are newspapers and other research data bases worth the relatively high on-line costs? In a general sense, the question is impossible to answer. How much value can be attached to a piece of research? Even if it leads to a contract or an investment return, can its worth be measured in cash? What percentage of the gain belongs to the research? And what about non-quantifiable uses? How much is it worth to save a forest from being cut down or a stream from pollution?

In a narrower sense, however, the question can be answered. Measure the cost of traveling to a library, and the time spent in the library doing research and waiting on clerks. Compare that against the time and cost spent on the data base. In most cases, the data base is cheaper. And it is almost always more thorough.

For example, in 1983 the magazine *Interface Age* estimated that a brief 40-minute trip to a library cost a total of $10.27 in terms of travel cost and the hourly wage of their writer who made the trip. Obtaining the equivalent information from The Source cost $2.61.

Lawyers tell me that a typical research project for their law clerks takes half a day at the library. The same search often can be conducted on a data base in less than 30 minutes. Not only is it cheaper, but they have the use of the clerk in other duties for the remainder of the day.

In my work, I rely heavily on newspaper libraries for research. I use newspapers of national scope, such as the New York *Times* or the Washington *Post,* and I use papers of regional and local scope, such as the Miami *Herald.* In pre-computer days, such research involved a trip downtown to the public library, parking costs and spending some three to six hours sifting through indexes and microfilm. On more complex stories, I might have to spend days and weeks to complete the research.

Those chores can now be done in minutes.

NEWSPAPERS FOR
THE BLIND

I haven't had the chance to try this system, but the people who make it swear it works. It's a system that will allow visually impaired users to hear newspapers, bulletin boards and other computer information that is written in English-language text.

Other than the brief bulletin-type news offered on television and radio, blind people don't have much access to current information. The few newspapers and magazines that are converted to cassettes or Braille for the blind are usually presenting news that is months old.

Now comes a method that would supply the news from Dow Jones News/Retrieval and other sources as soon as it breaks.

The program is Talking Transcend and was developed by Transend Corporation and an upstart company in Indiana named Computer Aids Corporation. The package incorporates Transend 2, a communications package for the Apple II series and IBM, a Transend modem and an Echo II speech synthesizer board, and has a list price of $645. If you already have a modem and communications package, you can buy the other components individually. The speech board has a list price of $150 and the Talking Transcend program $195.

After the user inserts the disk in the computer's drive, all information displayed on the video screen is spoken through the speech synthesizer. This includes information from data bases such as newspaper libraries or The Source. And it includes information typed in at the keyboard by the user.

The program can be used without the modem to simply guide blind users on what they are programming or displaying on their video display, whether it be spreadsheets, daily agendas, or popular adventure or strategy games which rely heavily on text.

The program is supposed to enable the blind to fully use consumer information services.

All documentation for Talking Transcend is recorded on cassette tapes. Further information can be obtained from Computer Aids Corp., 4929 S. Lafayette St., Fort Wayne, Indiana 46806. Telephone 219-456-2148.

I tend to believe this thing really works because the people who invented it and are marketing and using it are blind.

CHAPTER 16

Personal Services

THE INDUSTRY is about three years away from marketing my idea of a real computer. When it comes, I'll push a button to turn it on and it will say, "Good morning." (It knows morning because it has an internal clock.) "This is Hal. May I help you?"

I shouldn't say, "Good morning, Hal." The thing is a machine, right? But my wife, a full-grown woman, talks to a teddy bear. She also talks to the cabinet door when she closes it on her finger. So why shouldn't I talk to Hal?

"Hi Hal, I need to travel." And it will reply, "Sure thing, Dave." He knows my voice. There will be a very brief pause while Hal loads his travel program and asks, "Where would you like to go, Dave?" And I'll say, "Chicago," and he'll say, "When do you want to go?" And I'll reply, "Sunday," or "December 9" or "Tomorrow" and Hal will recognize all of them.

The machine also will know that the pattern of my previous flights indicates afternoon departures, coach class and the most forward aisle seat. Smoking or non-smoking doesn't matter. While I take a single sip of coffee, Hal dials up an airline schedule from a data base, checks the flights to Chicago for those closest to my preferences and then presents me with a list that includes fares.

I select one or more options. Hal quits the data base, connects to a travel agent or airline and makes my reservation, billing the cost to a pre-registered credit card. Hal then prints out the flight information so that I have something to take with me.

"Want a hotel, Dave?"

"Sure."

Hal now displays long lists of hotels, complete with prices, descriptions and *Mobil Travel Guide* ratings. Hal then lists restaurants.

Futuristic as it sounds, most of that can be done right now on The Source. It's not quite as easy. You can talk to The Source until you're blue. It won't do a thing. You use the keyboard. And the commands aren't quite as tolerant. "Tomorrow" means nothing to the computer. You need a date.

The Source will display national and international flight information via the Dittler Brothers data base, which lists the information as follows:

Domestic Air Schedules (USA, CAN, MEX)

FROM: MIAMI, FL

TO: CHICAGO, IL

DEPART	APT	ARRIVE	APT	FLIGHT	CLASS	DAYS	MEALS	PLANE	STOPS
08:45A		12:31P	O	EA 0218	FYBML	1234567	SLS	D9S	2
08:58A		11:35A	O	EA 0238	FYBML	1234567	L L	72S	1
09:45A		12:30P	M	QH 0044	YQK	1234567	L L	737	1
11:00A		01:00P	O	CL 0232	Y	1234567	S S	D8S	0
12:55P		02:46P	O	EA 0076	FYBML	1234567	L L	72S	0
12:55P		02:50P	O	DL 0942	FYBMV	1234567	L L	D8S	0
01:05P		03:05P	O	UA 0873	YBQM	1234567	L L	72S	0
06:29P		08:24P	O	EA 0078	FYBML	1234567	D D	L10	0
06:55P		09:00P	O	UA 0229	YBQM	1234567	D D	72S	0
07:35P		09:30P	M	QH 0004	YQK	1234567	D D	737	0
10:00P		12:01A	O	EA 0998	FYBML	1234567		72S	0

After listing the flight information, The Source can transfer us to Mobil Travel Services and display Chicago hotels. Here is a sample of a three-star hotel:

AMBASSADOR EAST.(Hotels & Inns) 1301 N State Parkway (60610), 2 mi N. 787-7200. 282 A/C rms. S, $105–$125; D, $125–$145; each addl, $18; suites, $195–$425; wkend packages; under 18 free. Crib, cot, free. Garage, $6. TV. Cafe (see PUMP ROOM). Rm serv. Bar, 11–2 AM. Ck-out, 1 PM. Coin lndry. Meeting rms. Shopping arcade. Concierge. Package store. Drugstore. Barber, beauty shop. Airport transportation. Most rms with oversize beds. Private patios, balconies in suites. Elegant. Cr cds: A, C, D, MC, V. Wheelchairs. Pets allowed. Spoken: German,Spanish,French,Italian.

Then we take a look at Mobil's Restaurant Guide, looking for four stars:

**** THE BAKERY. 2218 N Lincoln Ave (60614), 21/2 mi N. 472-6942. Hrs: 5–11 PM; Fri, Sat to 11:30 PM Res required. Closed Sun, Mon, hols. A/C. Continental cuisine. Wine. 5-course dinner (no menu), prix fixe, $21. Specialties: beef Wellington, roast duck. Own pastries. Street parking. Jacket required. Chef-owned. Cr cds: A, C, D, MC, V. Spoken: German,Spanish,French,Italian,Japanese.

Maybe there is even a five-star?

***** LE PERROQUET. 70 E Walton Pl (60611), 1 mi N. 944-7990. Hrs: noon–2 PM., 6–10 PM. Res required. Closed Sun, hols. A/C. French menu. Service bar. Wine list. Prix fixe. Lunch, $13.75 up; dinner, $38.50. Menu changes daily. Own pastries. Gracious dining; intimate and elegant. Jacket & tie required. Cr cds: A, C, D. Spoken: German,Spanish,French,Italian.

Finally, having been instructed to select a flight, a hotel and some restaurants, The Source can connect to The Travel Club, an on-line travel agency which makes the reservations, confirms them via SourceMail, then mails the tickets, if time permits, or else displays a "prepaid" number that allows us to pick up the tickets at the airport counter. All transactions are billed to a pre-registered credit card.

An almost identical service is offered by CompuServe. Its air schedules come from the Official Airline Guide (OAG) data base and list current fares, unlike Dittler Brothers, which omits the fares.

You pay, however, for the added convenience. Use of the OAG on CompuServe requires a premium payment of $21 per hour at night and $32 during prime business hours. I prefer to use Dittler Brothers and shop for fares by phone rather than pay the extra on-line costs.

CompuServe also has an on-line travel agency, Firstworld Travel Services. It handles more than 100 discounted tours and cruises all over the world and can make air and ground arrangements twenty-four hours a day. All tickets and confirmations can be delivered to the home, office, or to the airline counter at any airport.

At this writing, CompuServe has nothing comparable to the hotel and restaurant guides found on The Source. I travel a lot and find The Source's airline schedule and hotel and restaurant guides save money and make life better. The very first time I used The Source's airline schedule I was expecting to book on Eastern for a round trip between Boston and Miami. Eastern had the most flights but four other airlines flew that route and I checked their prices by phone. I ended up saving $200: the difference between Eastern's cheapest flight and a weekday special I found on another airline.

During 1983, my first full year using The Source, I estimate I saved more than $1,200 by shopping the flights listed on the data base.

I did the shopping on my own. I don't use travel agents. I've never had good luck with them. I've always been able to find better flights, cheaper flights on my own. Even back in the sixties. Other people have other experiences. They've done well with travel agents.

I tried the Source travel agency once. They were competent and friendly and booked a flight, car and hotel room. But I decided to check independently and found a flight that was $75 cheaper. Also, if you request reservations after 5 P.M. you may not receive confirmation until the end of the next working day. Of course, the agency's work on your behalf costs you nothing. They are compensated by a commission received from the airline, auto agency or hotel. But if you want to use a travel agent, I'd recommend a local one. At the least, you'll save the on-line costs.

I do recommend, however, the hotel and restaurant guides. As we've seen in the earlier chapter, they cover a wide, wide range of towns throughout the United States and Canada. They are a boon to anyone traveling in unfamiliar areas. Few people are likely to buy printed travel guides for every region. The computer listings are easier, quicker and more complete than the printed books.

I'd subscribe to The Source for the travel services alone. In addition to the benefits already noted, that little print-out of the schedules can rescue a lot of wasted hours. Many times I've finished work early in such places as Atlanta or New York or even small towns and found myself with an 8 P.M. flight and nothing to do for four hours. A peek at the printed schedule, a re-booking of airlines, a run to the gate and I was out of there. Often I've been back in Miami before that 8 P.M. flight took off and I would call and cancel my reservation myself.

The type of services available on data bases are virtually without limit, and range from help in house-hunting to help in keeping bees. One of the more interesting developments is the recent rise of computerized job-matching services.

One of these is Connexions of Cambridge, Massachusetts. For a one-time $15 fee, Connexions issues a password allowing the job hunter to log onto its main computer in New Hampshire. One can browse through detailed lists of job openings and enter a résumé into Connexions' computer by answering a series of questions. If an interesting job turns up, you ask Connexions to forward your résumé.

Typical of computerized job services, Connexions' openings are high-tech-oriented with emphasis on computer science, mechanical and chemical engineering, finance, marketing and sales. The company has been in business since 1982.

Another Massachusetts-headquartered service is JobNet of Bedford, Massachusetts, which came on line in July 1982. Unlike Connexions, which allows browsing by job hunters, JobNet keeps résumés without names and addresses for potential employers to look through. When they find a potential match, they ask JobNet to contact the person. JobNet's services are free for potential employees. You send them a résumé and JobNet enters it into its computer.

A combination of these services can be found on The Source, using the command: **EMPLOY.** That hooks us into "The Career Network," operated by Computer Search International of Baltimore, Maryland. It uses information from a network of professional recruiting firms scattered throughout the country. Begun in 1980, EMPLOY offers a wide range of openings ranging from accounting to utilities and is available only through The Source.

All three services are targeted at mid- to senior-level management openings. Confidentiality is a primary concern, and the services code résumés with numbers, so that employers don't learn a job hunter's name until the job hunter is absolutely sure of the employers' interest in the position.

Here is a list of the job categories found in EMPLOY:

ACCOUNTING	*ENERGY*	*PUBLISHING*
ADMIN/PERSONNEL	*ENGINEERING*	*REALESTATE*
ADVERTISING	*ENTERTAINMENT*	*RETAIL/WHOLE-TRADE*
AERONAUTICAL	*FINANCE*	*SALES*
AGRICULTURAL	*HOTEL/REST/FOOD*	*SERVICE*
ARTS	*INDUSTRIAL*	*SCIENCES*
BANKING/INVEST	*INSURANCE*	*SPORTS*
COMPUTERS	*LAW*	*TECHNICAL*
COMMUNICATIONS	*MANAGEMENT*	*TELECOMMUNICATIONS*
CONSTRUCTION	*MANUF/PROD*	*TRAVEL*
CONSULTING	*MARKETING*	*TRANSPORTATION*
ECONOMICS	*MATHEMATICS*	*UTILITIES*
EDUCATION	*MEDICAL/PHARM*	*MISCELLANEOUS*
ELECTRONICS		

I decided to take a look at a job in the publishing industry and found this:

THE PUBLISHING CATEGORY CURRENTLY HAS 3 JOBS.

AT THIS POINT, YOU MAY
    1—PRINT THESE ENTRIES,
    2—SELECT FURTHER FROM THIS DATA BASE BY SPECIFYING GEO-
      GRAPHIC LOCATION, SALARY RANGE DESIRED, OR WITH A
      KEYWORD SEARCH,
    3—LOCATE AND PRINT AN ENTRY BY REFERENCE NUMBER, OR
    4—RETURN TO SELECTION OF ANOTHER CATEGORY.

JOB 1 OF 3 SALARY RANGE: $20,000–$29,000 LOCATION: MASSACHU-
SETTS JOB TITLE: TECHNICAL EDITOR TYPE BUSINESS: COMPUTER
MAGAZINE SIZE OF BUSINESS: FORTUNE 200 PRODUCT: MAGA-
ZINE EDUCATION: BA DESCRIPTION OF JOB: WRITING, EDITING,

AND SOLICITING STORIES AND IDEAS FOR STORIES IN FAST-MOV-
ING HIGH TECH COMPUTER PUBLISHING ENVIRONMENT. EXPE-
RIENCE DESIRED—COMMENTS: SEVERAL YEARS IN PUBLISHING,
HIGH-TECH EXPERIENCE PREFERRED. FAMILIARITY WITH DEC
MICROS DESIRABLE. MUST LIVE IN OR RELOCATE TO THE BOS-
TON/128 AREA.

CONTACT CSI079 VIA ELECTRONIC MAIL, REFERENCE CSI079-GEP
109

JOB 2 OF 3 SALARY RANGE: $30,000–$39,000 LOCATION: CONNECTI-
CUT JOB TITLE: CREATIVE MANAGER TYPE BUSINESS: MFG MAN-
UFACTURING SIZE OF BUSINESS: LARGE-NATIONALLY KNOWN
PRODUCT: RETAIL MACHINERY EDUCATION: ANY DEGREE DE-
SCRIPTION OF JOB: IN CHARGE OF ALL ART COPYWRITING, LAY-
OUT, PHOTOGRAPHY, COLOR AND PRINTING OF EXTENSIVE
BUSINESS TO BUSINESS CATALOGUES. RELOCATION PAID. EXPE-
RIENCE DESIRED—COMMENTS: 4 PLUS YEARS MARKETING, COP-
YWRITING, LAYOUT, PHOTOGRAPHY AND SUPERVISION. TOP
SKILLS IN ALL ABOVE.

CONTACT CSI107 VIA ELECTRONIC MAIL, REFERENCE CSI107-AP102

JOB 3 OF 3 SALARY RANGE: $30,000–$39,000 LOCATION: MASSACHU-
SETTS JOB TITLE: TECHNICAL INSTRUCTOR TYPE BUSINESS: ENGI-
NEERING SIZE OF BUSINESS: FORTUNE 500 PRODUCT: ATE EDUCA-
TION: BSEE OR EQUIV. DESCRIPTION OF JOB: INSTRUCT
CUSTOMERS ON HOW TO PROGRAM AND USE ATE EQUIP. WILL
ALSO TEACH THE HARDWARE USE OF EQUIP. THERE WILL BE
SOME TECHNICAL WRITING AND COURSE DEVELOPMENT. EXPE-
RIENCE DESIRED—COMMENTS: 2 TO 3 YEARS CLASS ROOM EXP.
TEACHING BOTH HARDWARE SOFTWARE

CONTACT CSI079 VIA ELECTRONIC MAIL, REFERENCE CSI079-GFM
114

This chapter began with a fantasy about the ideal computer, Hal. We
speak to Hal. Hal speaks to us. Things get done. "Hal, take me shopping."

In the future, the shopping abilities of a computer may be its single
most valuable asset. Unlike printed catalogs or printed ads, computers
can list tens of thousands of items for sale, give their descriptions and
theoretically display color pictures. Prices can be changed hour by hour.

One of the more interesting ventures is Grocery Express, a San Francisco
delivery service which, for about $3 depending upon your distance from
their store, lets you go on line with their computer, review a shopping
list, place your order and have it delivered the next day. It beats the
hell out of the one to three hours and more we spend every week lugging
groceries to the house.

But computer shopping is much bigger than just Grocery Express. The videotex services we mentioned earlier, in Miami, Los Angeles and Chicago, offer local shopping at local department stores via computer.

And there is a national service called Comp-U-Store which works quite well. It is accessible through The Source, CompuServe, Dow Jones and its own network of local phone numbers and 800-area-code long-distance numbers.

You can dial up Comp-U-Store on the information services and join on line, provided you have a major credit card. As a member, you may obtain information on product descriptions, current model numbers and price quotations, and buy items at substantial discounts.

The prices almost always are lower than normal retail stores' and often as low or lower than discount houses'. The prices quoted on Comp-U-Store include all taxes, delivery and other costs.

Comp-U-Store markets over 50,000 products, including all major appliances such as air conditioners and washer/dryers, cameras and optical equipment, car equipment and sometimes even cars, flatware and crystal, luggage, sports equipment, stereo and audio equipment, television and other video equipment, furniture, telephone and computer equipment and accessories, and miscellaneous items, such as clocks, radios, circular saws, power drills and pianos.

Comp-U-Store isn't a warehouse store but instead a broker that arranges for distributors and manufacturers to ship directly to you. Comp-U-Store promises to seek the vendor which provides the best price and service to your geographic area.

In addition to the normal discounted products, the store offers two other services—both of which are fun. One is a bargain basement with a limited number of products offered at even further reduced prices. The second is a weekly auction in which a limited number of products are put on the block and the highest bidder wins.

The auction feature, like all auctions, is weird. I have seen items go at rock-bottom prices. But I have also seen people bid and buy at prices 30 to 50 percent higher than they'd pay by ordering through the normal Comp-U-Store process.

I've found two disadvantages with Comp-U-Store. First, the product descriptions are too skimpy. I've usually had to look in printed catalogs to find fuller descriptions of what I think Comp-U-Store is offering. I then buy from either the printed catalog or Comp-U-Store, depending on price and speed of delivery. The meager descriptions offered by Comp-U-Store are a definite hindrance to buying.

Another hindrance is the delivery time. Comp-U-Store warns buyers that delivery of an item may take three to five weeks. Now, that is a long time to wait. Particularly for us impulse buyers.

Nevertheless, in early January 1984, Mary and I decided to buy a microwave oven. The decision was a given. What remained was price and delivery terms. At the time, Burdines, a large quality department store in Miami, was advertising a top-rated Amana RR700 on sale at $383. It was marked down from $479. I wanted delivery because the thing weighed 84 pounds. The total price to my door, including delivery fee and sales tax, would be $408.19.

Because we weren't in a hurry, I decided to check Comp-U-Store's prices. I found the same machine and ordered it. Three weeks later to the day, it was delivered to our kitchen from a dealer in New Jersey. The total cost was $329.01. We had saved $79.18.

In such normal consumer transactions as shopping for appliances, air fares or other goods or services, computers can save you literally hundreds and even thousands of dollars. Forget the money you might make in stock market investments and other risk ventures. Just think of the money you can save as a consumer.

Another Comp-U-Store feature is CARS. When I saw the category CARS, I wondered how they could sell a car via a computer. You can't charge a car to a credit card. At least not to mine. A motor scooter, or a pair of water skis maybe. But not a car.

I dialed it and what I found was that for a five-dollar fee you will get price quotes on all American cars and several foreign models. Comp-U-Store mails a form in which you specify the options wanted on the car. They'll return with a quote guaranteed to be only $125 above dealer costs. The car will be sold by a dealer in your area and all you have to do is go get it.

Here's what the display looks like on an excellent buy which will save you between $500 and $800 on a quality computer:

Computers

Mfg :ZENITH   Model:ZF10021
List : 2899.00   Srchg :
FDC: 2372.04   Color :
Save : 526.96

Description

DESKTOP COMPUTER FEATURES
TYPEWRITER KEYBOARD, MONOCHROME
MONITOR, INTERNAL MEMORY OF 128K
RAM (EXPANDABLE TO 768K) AND ONE
5-1/4" DISK DRIVE. ALSO HAS TWO
RS-232C PARALLEL INTERFACE PORTS
Want to order? (Y or N)

CONCLUSION

Is It Worth It?

WE NOW COME TO THE END of our survey of what's out there and how to get it. I've deliberately not examined the many sophisticated uses available to businesses, universities and mainframe systems. That is a separate subject. In many ways, it's as different from what we've discussed as two languages such as Italian and Spanish. They have common sources and assumptions, but to understand one is not necessarily to understand the other. For those who are interested in more technical uses of telecommunications, a good starting place is a college or public library.

As for the data bases and systems we have discussed, it's up to you to assess whether it's worth your time and money to go forward.

Dialing up the data works for me, in both a professional and a private sense. Professionally, I receive assignments and other job communications from my employer via electronic mail. This allows me to avoid even visiting an office. And I use the data bases extensively for research.

It also saves money for my employers because it is vastly cheaper to transmit story files on my personal computer than to use Telex or Western Union or some other commercial service.

It saves money for me personally because I can shop around for hotels, airlines, even microwave ovens.

And it's fun. Jumping on a local bulletin board is like having a private mail delivery whenever you want it.

Your assessments of the uses of telecommunications may be different. There are those who may think it's a real yawn. But for the rest of you, I hope this book has been of some help.

(Signed) Dave Chandler, Source ID ST9502.

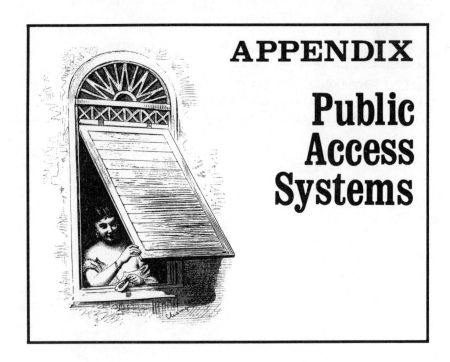

APPENDIX

Public Access Systems

/-

BULLETIN BOARD AND FILE TRANSFER SYSTEMS

Compliments of Peoples' Message System, Santee, CA
(619) 561-7277
Compiled and maintained by Bill Blue
(with a lot of help from his friends)

>All phone numbers are subject to change<

The PMS Santee bulletin board is the nation's central directory for bulletin board phone numbers. PMS Santee is a private board sponsored by Marilla Corporation, specialists in personal computer communications software development, and by Datel Systems, Inc., a retailer of personal computer software and hardware of all types. PMS Santee lists bulletin boards alphabetically, by area code and by type of equipment.

The system, operated by Sysop Bill Blue, consists of a 48K Apple II computer with the D. C. Hayes Micromodem card and specially designed software. For the technically inclined, disk storage is supported by one Persci model 277 dual drive operating under Apple DOS 3.2. The drive is interfaced to the Apple by a Sorrento Valley Associates dual density controller card. Each disk is capable of approximately 505K of storage, giving the system a total of 1.1 megabytes of system and user files.

Regular updates of this list may be found by accessing CompuServe, entering the command mode and typing MAUG XA4; by accessing The Source, entering the command mode and typing PUBLIC 112; or by accessing the Santee board directly at (619) 561-7277. PMS Santee charges no fee for the use of its board.

ABBS refers to Apple Bulletin Board System. It runs exclusively on the Apple II, although any type of computer may call an ABBS board.

BULLET-80 refers to software running on Radio Shack TRS-80 machines, but people with all types of computers use the boards.

CBBS stands for Computer Bulletin Board System, which was one of the earliest systems for public boards. The software was donated by Ward Christiansen, a telecommunications legend.

FORUM-80 runs on TRS-80 computers but welcomes all computers.

NET-WORKS runs on the Apple II but supports all callers.

PMS stands for Public Message System. It runs on Apple II computers but accepts calls from any computer or terminal and is perhaps the easiest of all systems for first-time users.

RCP/M runs on nearly any computer that uses the CP/M operating system.

The above are the most commonly used systems. There are many other systems, such as the Message-80 for Radio Shack Models I and II, and PBBS, run by Commodore Pet computers. Almost all boards, regardless of name, can be accessed by almost all computers or terminals.

KEY TO SYMBOLS:

· Listed systems' hours of operation:
  * denotes mostly 24-hour 7-day operation
  + denotes 8–12 hour DAYTIME operation ONLY
  − denotes 8–12 hour NIGHTTIME operation ONLY

· New listings or changes:
  ! denotes a new system, a new number for an existing system or a new list entry

· All systems listed support Bell 103a 300 bits per second:
  $ also supports VADIC (3400 series) 1200 Bps.
  & also supports Bell 212A 1200 Bps.
  % also supports BAUDOT operation (usually 45.5 Bps.)

· System categories:
  #1 denotes original or "home" system of that type
  dd. denotes game-oriented messages or game playing
  dl. denotes download/upload capabilities, a program exchange system
  ml. denotes mail/information exchange only
  rb. denotes call, let ring once and call back
  rl. denotes religious orientation
  so. denotes sexually oriented messages

  → List now begins in alpha-numeric order by type:

ABBS Akron Digital Group, Akron, OH .... (216) 745-7855*
ABBS Analog, Port Coquitlam, BC, CN .... (604) 941-0041*
ABBS Apple Crate I, Seattle, WA .... !(206) 872-6789
ABBS Byte Shop, Fort Lauderdale, FL .... (305) 486-2983—
ABBS Byte Shop, Miami, FL............................... (305) 261-3639—
ABBS CODE, Glen Ellyn, IL.............................. (312) 882-2926*
ABBS Colortron Computer, Racine, WI .... (414) 637-9990*
ABBS Compumart, Ottawa, Ontario, CN .... (613) 725-2243
ABBS Computer Room, Kalamazoo, MI .... (616) 382-0101
ABBS Gamemaster, Chicago, IL .... (312) 475-4884*
ABBS Image Base, Long Beach, CA....................... !(213) 597-0064*
ABBS Ketchikan, AK.................................... (907) 225-6789
ABBS LINX, Lincoln, NE .... (402) 476-1177*dl.
ABBS Nessy Game System, Itasca, IL.................... (312) 773-3308*
ABBS Nessy Flynn's BBS, Crystal Lake, IL................ (815) 455-2406
ABBS New York, NY .... (516) 473-1005*
ABBS New York, NY .... (212) 877-7703*
ABBS Omaha, NE...................................... (402) 339-7809
ABBS Pacific Palisades, Los Angeles, CA.................. (213) 459-6400
ABBS Peoria, IL...................................... (309) 692-6502
ABBS Phoenix, AZ .... (602) 898-0891
ABBS Pirates Cove, Long Island, NY .... (516) 698-4008
ABBS Rogers Park, Chicago, IL .... (312) 973-2227
ABBS Software Sorcery, Herndon, VA .... &(703) 471-0610*
ABBS South of Market, San Francisco, CA .... (415) 469-8111 so.
ABBS Teledunjon III, Dallas, TX .... (214) 960-7654*dd.
ABBS The Pulse, Dallas, TX .... (214) 631-7747*so.
ABBS Turnersville, NJ................................. (609) 228-1149
ABBS Vancouver, BC, CN .... (604) 437-7001
ABBS Vermont, Essex Junction, VT .... (802) 879-4981*
ABBS West Palm Beach, FL .... (305) 848-3802

ACS Arlington Heights, IL .... #1(312) 392-2403
ACS Chicago, IL...................................... (312) 445-1130

A-C-C-E-S-S Annapolis, MD .... (301) 267-7666*
A-C-C-E-S-S Phoenix, AZ .... (602) 275-6644
A-C-C-E-S-S Phoenix, AZ.............................. &(602) 957-4428*
A-C-C-E-S-S Scottsdale, AZ .... (602) 998-9411*
A-C-C-E-S-S Wyckoff, NJ.............................. (201) 891-7441*

AMIS A.R.C.A.D.E., Sterling Heights, MI................. (313) 978-8087*
AMIS Clarendon Hills, IL.............................. (312) 789-3610*
AMIS GRAFEX, Cupertino, CA.......................... (408) 253-5216
AMIS G.R.A.S.S., Grand Rapids, MI..................... (616) 241-1971*
AMIS IBBBS, San Jose, CA............................. (408) 298-6930
AMIS M.A.C.E., Detroit, MI .... #1(313) 589-0996*

AMIS T.A.B.B.S., Sunnyvale, CA . . . . (408) 942-6975
ARMUDIC Washington, DC . . . . #1(202) 276-8342
ARMUDIC Computer Age, Balti more, MD . . . . (301) 587-2132

BBS IBM Hostcomm Atlanta, GA. . . . . (404) 252-4146
BBS IBM Hostcomm Fairfax, VA. . . . . (703) 978-9592*
BBS IBM Hostcomm Fairfax, VA. . . . . (703) 591-5120*
BBS IBM Hostcomm Fairfax, VA. . . . . (703) 425-9452*
BBS IBM Hostcomm Houston, TX . . . . (713) 890-0310*
BBS IBM Hostcomm Springfield, VA. . . . . (703) 425-7229*
BBS IBM Hostcomm Toronto, Ontario, CN. . . . . (416) 499-7023*
BBS IBM PC Annandale, VA . . . . (703) 560-0979*
BBS IBM PC Atlanta, GA. . . . . (404) 928-3005
BBS IBM PC Atlanta, GA. . . . . (404) 252-9438*
BBS IBM PC Beltsville, MD. . . . . (301) 937-4339*
BBS IBM PC Bethesda, MD. . . . . (301) 460-0538*
BBS IBM PC Charlotte, NC . . . . (704) 365-4311*
BBS IBM PC Computer Society, Boston, MA . . . . (617) 353-9312—
BBS IBM PC Culver City, CA. . . . . &(213) 649-1489*
BBS IBM PC Dale City, VA . . . . (703) 680-5220*
BBS IBM PC Gaithersburg, MD . . . . (301) 251-6293*
BBS IBM PC Great Falls, VA. . . . . !&(703) 759-5049*
BBS IBM PC Madison, WI . . . . (608) 262-4939*
BBS IBM PC Niles, IL. . . . . (312) 991-8887*
BBS IBM PC Rockville, MD . . . . (301) 949-8848*
BBS IBM PC Vienna, VA. . . . . (703) 560-7803*
BBS IBM PCmodem Chicago, IL . . . . &(312) 882-4227*
BBS IBM PCmodem Chicago, IL. . . . . (312) 376-7598*

BULLET-80 Boston, MA. . . . . &(617) 266-7789*
BULLET-80 Chesterland, OH . . . . (216) 729-2769
BULLET-80 Danbury, CT. . . . . #1(203) 744-4644
BULLET-80 El Paso, TX. . . . . !(915) 565-9903*
BULLET-80 Fayetteville, GA. . . . . (404) 461-9686
BULLET-80 Hattiesburg, MS . . . . (601) 264-2361*
BULLET-80 Holstein, IA. . . . . (712) 368-2651
BULLET-80 Langhorne, PA . . . . (215) 364-2180
BULLET-80 New York, NY. . . . . (718) 740-5680*
BULLET-80 Orange County, Anaheim, CA. . . . . (714) 952-2110
BULLET-80 Pirate Place, VA. . . . . (703) 734-1387*
BULLET-80 Seymour, CT . . . . (203) 888-7952
BULLET-80 Springfield, IL. . . . . (217) 529-1113
BULLET-80 Waterford, MI . . . . (313) 628-4350*

CBBS Aurora Computer Peripherals, Aurora, CO . . . . (312) 897-9037*
CBBS Baton Rouge, LA. . . . . (504) 273-3116*
CBBS Boston, MA . . . . (617) 646-3610*

CBBS Cedar Rapids, IA . . . . (319) 364-0811*
CBBS Chicago, IL. . . . . #1(312) 545-8086*
CBBS CPEUG/ICST Gaithersburg, MD . . . . (301) 948-5717
CBBS Lambda, Berkeley, CA . . . . (415) 658-2919 so.
CBBS Lawrence General Hospital, Boston, MA . . . . (617) 683-2119
CBBS LICA LIMBS, Long Island, NY . . . . (516) 561-6590*
CBBS London, England (European standard) . . . . (044) 1-399-2136
CBBS Long Island, NY . . . . (516) 334-3134*
CBBS MAUDE Milwaukee, WI . . . . (414) 241-8364*
CBBS NW, Portland, OR . . . . (503) 646-5510*
CBBS PACC, Pittsburgh, PA . . . . (412) 822-7176*
CBBS Prince George, BC, CN . . . . (604) 562-9515
CBBS Proxima, Berkeley, CA. . . . . (415) 357-1130
CBBS RAMS, Rochester, NY . . . . (716) 244-9531
CBBS Rosemont, MN. . . . . (612) 423-5016
CBBS St. Petersburg, FL. . . . . (813) 866-9945*
CBBS Strictly Software, Honolulu, HI . . . . (808) 944-0562
CBBS TSG, Tucson, AZ. . . . . (602) 574-0327*
CBBS Ward and Randy's, Chicago, IL . . . . (312) 259-8086

COMNET-80 Akron, OH. . . . . &(216) 645-0827*
COMNET-80 Las Vegas, NV . . . . &(702) 870-9986
COMNET-80 Mt. Clemens, MI . . . . &(313) 465-9531
COMNET-80 North Wales, PA . . . . (215) 855-3809
COMNET-80 Riverside, CA . . . . &(714) 359-3189
COMNET-80 Riverside, CA. . . . . &(714) 877-2253
COMNET-80 Wichita Falls, TX. . . . . (817) 767-5847

CONFERENCE-TREE Berkeley, CA . . . . (408) 475-7101
CONFERENCE-TREE Computerland, Honolulu, HI. . . . . (808) 487-2001*
CONFERENCE-TREE Flagship, Rockaway, NJ . . . . (201) 627-5151*
CONFERENCE-TREE Hayward, CA. . . . . (415) 538-3580
CONFERENCE-TREE Kelp Bed, Los Angeles, CA. . . . . (213) 372-4800
CONFERENCE-TREE Minneapolis, MN. (612) 854-9691
CONFERENCE-TREE Phoenix, AZ. . . . . (602) 931-1829*
CONFERENCE-TREE San Francisco, CA . . . . #1(415) 861-6489
CONFERENCE-TREE Santa Monica, CA . . . . (213) 394-1505
CONFERENCE-TREE Sausalito, CA. . . . . (415) 332-8115

CONNECTION-80 Centereach, NY. . . . . (516) 588-5836
CONNECTION-80 Denver, CO . . . . (303) 690-4566*
CONNECTION-80 Fremont, CA . . . . (415) 651-4147*
CONNECTION-80 Gaithersburg, MD. . . . . (301) 840-8588*
CONNECTION-80 JACS, Jacksonville, FL. . . . . !(904) 353-5227*
CONNECTION-80 Lansing, MI. . . . . (517) 339-3367
CONNECTION-80 Laval BELE, Laval, Quebec, CN . . . . (514) 622-1274*
CONNECTION-80 Manhattan, NY . . . . (212) 991-1664

CONNECTION-80 Orlando, FL . . . . (305) 644-8327*
CONNECTION-80 Peterborough, NH . . . . (603) 924-7920
CONNECTION-80 Tampa, FL . . . . (813) 977-0989
CONNECTION-80 Winter Garden, FL. (305) 894-1886*
CONNECTION-80 Woodhaven, NY . . . . (718) 441-3755*

DIAL-YOUR-MATCH #3 . . . . (912) 233-0863 so.
DIAL-YOUR-MATCH #4 . . . . (213) 783-2305 so.
DIAL-YOUR-MATCH #8, San Francisco, CA . . . . (415) 467-2588 so.
DIAL-YOUR-MATCH #9. . . . . (213) 345-1047 so.
DIAL-YOUR-MATCH #11, Carlsbad, CA . . . . (619) 434-4600*so.
DIAL-YOUR-MATCH #12, Houston, TX. . . . . (713) 556-1531*so.
DIAL-YOUR-MATCH #14. . . . . (201) 272-3686 so.
DIAL-YOUR-MATCH #16 . . . . (206) 256-6624 so.
DIAL-YOUR-MATCH #17. . . . . (415) 991-4911 so.
DIAL-YOUR-MATCH #18. . . . . (617) 334-6369 so.
DIAL-YOUR-MATCH #20 . . . . (919) 362-0676 so. – Good '84
DIAL-YOUR-MATCH #21, Freehold, NJ . . . . (201) 462-0435 so.
DIAL-YOUR-MATCH #22 . . . . (213) 990-6830 so.
DIAL-YOUR-MATCH #23, Omaha, NE . . . . (402) 571-8942 so.
DIAL-YOUR-MATCH #26, Clovis, CA. . . . . (209) 298-1328 so.
DIAL-YOUR-MATCH #37, Flint, MI. . . . . (313) 736-1398 so.
DIAL-YOUR-MATCH #38, Austin, TX . . . . (512) 451-8747 so.
DIAL-YOUR-MATCH #39, Chicago, IL . . . . (312) 243-1046 so.

FORUM-80 Augusta, GA. . . . . (803) 279-5392
FORUM-80 Cleveland, OH. . . . . &(216) 486-4176
FORUM-80 El Paso, TX. . . . . (915) 755-1000*
FORUM-80 Fort Lauderdale, FL . . . . (305) 772-4444*
FORUM-80 Las Vegas, NV . . . . (702) 362-3609*
FORUM-80 Linden, NJ. . . . . (201) 486-2956*
FORUM-80 Medford, OR. . . . . (503) 535-6883*
FORUM-80 Medical, Memphis, TN. . . . . (901) 276-8196*
FORUM-80 Monmouth, Brielle, NJ. . . . . (201) 528-6623*
FORUM-80 Montgomery, AL. . . . . (205) 272-5069
FORUM-80 Prince William County, VA. . . . . (703) 670-5881*
FORUM-80 San Mateo, CA. . . . . &(415) 348-2139
FORUM-80 Seattle, WA. . . . . (206) 723-3282
FORUM-80 Sierra Vista, AZ . . . . (602) 458-3850*
FORUM-80 Westford, MA . . . . (617) 692-3973
FORUM-80 Wichita, KS . . . . &(316) 682-2113*

GREENE MACHINE Chicago, IL. (312) 622-4442 so.
GREENE MACHINE Corsair, WPB, FL . . . . (305) 968-8653
GREENE MACHINE Golden State BBS, Novato, CA. . . . . . . (415) 897-2783
GREENE MACHINE New Orleans, LA . . . . !(504) 279-3832*
GREENE MACHINE Riverside, CA . . . . (714) 354-8004

GREENE MACHINE Rome, NY......................... (315) 337-7720
GREENE MACHINE Yuma, AZ...................... !&(602) 726-7533*

HBBS Heath/Zenith, Grand Rapids, MI .... &(616) 531-0890
HBBS MOG-UR, Granada Hills, CA .... &(213) 366-1238*

MCMS C.A.M.S. Chicago, IL........................ #1&(312) 927-1020*
MCMS Goliath, Minneapolis, MN......................... (612) 753-3082
MCMS J.A.M.S. Lockport, IL............................. (815) 838-1020*
MCMS NC Software, Minneapolis, MN.................... (612) 533-1957*
MCMS P.C.M.S. Wheaton, IL.......................... &(312) 462-7560*
MCMS WACO Hot Line, Schaumburg, IL (pvt.).............. (312) 351-4374*
MCMS Word Exchange, Springfield, IL .... (217) 753-4309*

NET-WORKS ABC, Kansas City, MO....................... (816) 483-2526
NET-WORKS Adventure's Inn, Lake Forest, IL.............. (312) 295-7284*
NET-WORKS AGS, Augusta, GA .... (404) 733-3461*
NET-WORKS Apple Gumbo, Shreveport, LA .... !(318) 861-1012*
NET-WORKS Apple Juice, Darien, IL..................... (312) 685-9573
NET-WORKS Apple Net, Chicago, IL..................... (312) 963-5384
NET-WORKS Apple-Technical, Chicago, IL .... (312) 935-3091
NET-WORKS Armadillo, Grand Forks, ND................. (701) 746-4959
NET-WORKS Assembly Line, Louisville, KY .... (502) 459-5531—
NET-WORKS Asylum, Edwardsville, IL .... (618) 692-0742
NET-WORKS Baud-ville, Louisville, KY .... (502) 423-0695—
NET-WORKS Beach BBS, Pensacola, FL.................... (904) 932-8271
NET-WORKS Big Apple, Miami, FL....................... (305) 948-8000
NET-WORKS Briar-Net, Houston, TX..................... (713) 782-5706*
NET-WORKS Brooklyn, NY .... (212) 410-0949
NET-WORKS C.A.M.S., Decatur, IL...................... (217) 429-4738*
NET-WORKS Charleston, WV .... (304) 345-8280
NET-WORKS Chipmunk, Hinsdale, IL.................... (312) 323-3741*
NET-WORKS Coin Games, Los Angeles, CA .... (213) 336-5535
NET-WORKS Computer Library, New Orleans, LA .... !(504) 885-2391*
NET-WORKS Computer Market, Honolulu, HI .... (808) 524-6668—
NET-WORKS Computer Pro, Fort Worth, TX .... (817) 732-1787
NET-WORKS Computer World, Los Angeles, CA .... (213) 859-0894*
NET-WORKS Dante's Inferno, New Orleans, LA .... !(504) 392-4156*
NET-WORKS Dayton, OH............................... (513) 223-3672
NET-WORKS Eclectic Computer Sys., Dallas, TX............. (214) 239-5842
NET-WORKS Fourth Dimension, St. Louis, MO .... (314) 532-4652
NET-WORKS GBBS Metro Detroit, MI.................. !(313) 455-4227 so.
NET-WORKS Greenfield, IN .... (317) 326-4152*
NET-WORKS Hawaii................................... (808) 524-6652
NET-WORKS Hawaii Connection, Honolulu, HI .... (808) 423-1593*
NET-WORKS Jolly Roger, Houston, TX .... (713) 468-0174*
NET-WORKS Livingston, NJ .... (201) 994-9620*

NET-WORKS MAGIE, Galesburg, IL .... (309) 342-7178
NET-WORKS Magnetic Fantasies, Los Angeles, CA .... (213) 388-5198
NET-WORKS MicroBBS, Chelmsford, MA .... (603) 889-4330
NET-WORKS Micro Ideas, Glenview, IL .... (312) 998-5066
NET-WORKS Mines of Moria, Houston, TX .... (713) 871-8577*
NET-WORKS N A G S, Alton, IL .... (618) 466-9497
NET-WORKS Nick Naimo, Newburgh, IN .... #1(812) 858-5405
NET-WORKS Pirate's Harbor, Boston, MA .... (617) 720-3600
NET-WORKS Pirate's Harbor, Cambridge, MA .... (617) 494-1985
NET-WORKS Pirate's Lodge, New City, NY .... (914) 634-1268
NET-WORKS Portsmouth, NH .... (603) 436-3461
NET-WORKS RJNET, Warnville, IL .... (312) 393-4755
NET-WORKS Softworx, West Los Angeles, CA .... (213) 473-2754
NET-WORKS The Dark Realm, Houston, TX .... (713) 333-2309*dd.
NET-WORKS The Shadow World, Houston, TX .... (713) 777-8608*
NET-WORKS The Silver Tongue, St. Joseph, MO .... (816) 232-3153
NET-WORKS The System, Houston, TX .... (713) 785-7996—
NET-WORKS The Weekender, Houston, TX .... (713) 492-8700*
NET-WORKS Toronto, Ontario, CN .... (416) 445-6696*
NET-WORKS Warlock's Castle, St. Louis, MO .... (618) 345-6638
NET-WORKS Zachary*Net, Houston, TX .... (713) 933-7353*

ONLINE Dickinsons Movie Guide, Mission, KS .... (913) 432-5544*
ONLINE Omega, Chicago, IL .... (312) 648-4867*
ONLINE Saba, San Diego, CA .... (619) 692-1961*

P.dBMS-Lakeside, CA .... $&!(619) 561-7271*ml.

PET BBS AVC Comline, Indianapolis, IN .... (317) 255-5435*
PET BBS Commodore, Chicago, IL .... (312) 397-0871*
PET BBS Commodore, Largo, FL .... (813) 391-5219+
PET BBS PSI WordPro, Ontario, CN .... #1(416) 624-5431*
PET BBS S.E.W.P.U.G., Racine, WI .... (414) 554-9520*
PET BBS SE Wyoming PUG .... (307) 637-6045*
PET BBS TPUG, Toronto, Ontario, CN .... (416) 223-2625*

PMS—**IF**, Anaheim, CA .... (714) 772-8868*
PMS—Anchorage, AK .... (907) 344-8558
PMS—Apple Bits, Kansas City, MO .... (816) 252-0232*
PMS—Century 23, Las Vegas, NV .... (702) 878-9106*
PMS—Chicago, IL .... (312) 373-8057*
PMS—Cincinnati, OH .... (513) 671-2753
PMS—Computer City, Danvers, MA .... (617) 774-7516
PMS—Computer Merchant, San Diego, CA .... (619) 582-9557*ml.
PMS—Computer Solutions, Eugene, OR .... (503) 689-2655*
PMS—Datel Systems Inc., San Diego, CA .... (619) 271-8613*
PMS—Downers Grove/SRT, Downers Grove, IL .... (312) 964-6513

PMS—Ed Tech, San Diego, CA............................. (619) 265-3428
PMS—Ellicott City, MD .... (301) 465-3176
PMS—Escondido, CA...................................... (619) 746-0667—
PMS—Floppy House, San Diego, CA........................ !(619) 579-7036*
PMS—Fort Smith Comp. Club, Fort Smith, AR .... (501) 646-0197
PMS—Gulfcoast, Freeport, TX .... (409) 233-7943*
PMS—I.A.C., Lake Forest, IL .... (312) 295-6926*
PMS—Indianapolis, IN .... (317) 787-5486*
PMS—Kid's Message System, San Diego, CA .... (619) 578-2646*
PMS—Logic Inc., Toronto, Ontario, CN.................... (416) 447-8458*
PMS—Los Angeles, CA .... (213) 331-3574*
PMS—Massillon, OH...................................... (216) 832-8392*
PMS—McGraw-Hill Books, New York, NY................... (212) 997-2488
PMS—Minneapolis, MN .... (612) 929-6699*
PMS—O.A.C., Woodland Hills, CA......................... (213) 346-1849*
PMS—Pikesville, MD..................................... (301) 653-3413
PMS—Pleasanton, CA .... (415) 462-7419*
PMS—Portland, OR .... (503) 245-2536*
PMS—Portola Valley, CA .... (415) 851-3453*
PMS—RAUG, Akron, OH .... (216) 867-7463* TLX 377-5186*
PMS—Rutgers Univ. Microlab, Piscataway, NJ............... (201) 932-3887
PMS—San Marcos, CA.................................... (619) 727-7500*
PMS—Santa Cruz, Aptos, CA............................. (408) 688-9629*
PMS—Santee, CA .... #1(619) 561-7277*ml.
PMS—SEB Computer, Jacksonville, FL..................... !(904) 743-7050
PMS—Software Unltd, Kenmore, WA .... (206) 486-2368*
PMS—Twin Cities, Minneapolis, MN .... (612) 929-8966

PSBBS Baltimore, MD................................... (301) 994-0399*
PSBBS Washington, DC.................................. (202) 337-4694*

RATS Wenonah, NJ..................................... (609) 468-5293
RATS Wenonah, NJ #2 .... (609) 853-8268

RCP/M A. B. Dick Co., Niles, IL .... &(312) 647-7636*
RCP/M Anchorage, AK................................... (907) 337-1984—
RCP/M Arlington, VA .... (703) 536-3769—
RCP/M Barstow, CA.................................... $(619) 256-3914*
RCP/M Beaverton, OR.................................. (503) 641-7276*
RCP/M Blue Ridge, Missouri City, TX .... !(713) 438-2247*
RCP/M Boulder, CO .... (303) 499-9169—
RCP/M Bridgeport, IL .... (312) 326-4392*
RCP/M CBBS ANAHUG, Anaheim, CA .... (714) 774-7860*
RCP/M CBBS Columbus, OH............................. (614) 272-2227*
RCP/M CBBS Dallas, TX .... (214) 931-8274—
RCP/M CBBS Frog Hollow, Vancouver, BC, CN .... (604) 937-0906*
RCP/M CBBS Maxicom, Farmers Branch, TX............. &$!(214) 241-1939*

RCP/M CBBS Maxicom, Line 2 . . . . !(214) 247-5307
RCP/M CBBS MICOM, Melbourne, VIC, Australia 61 3 762-5088*
RCP/M CBBS Pasadena, CA . . . . (213) 799-1632*
RCP/M CBBS Technical, Detroit, MI. &(313) 846-6127*
RCP/M Chuck Forsberg, OR. . . . . $&(503) 621-3193*
RCP/M Colossal Oxgate, San Jose, CA . . . . (408) 263-2588
RCP/M CUG-NODE, PA State College . . . . (814) 238-4857*
RCP/M CUG-NOTE, Denver, CO . . . . (303) 781-4937*
RCP/M Dave McCrady, Edmonton, Alberta, CN. . . . . $&!(403) 454-6093*
RCP/M DBASE, San Jose, CA . . . . (408) 378-8733*
RCP/M EI Division, Argonne, IL. . . . . (312) 972-6979
RCP/M Flanders, NJ . . . . &(201) 584-9227*
RCP/M Geneseo, IL. . . . . (309) 944-5455
RCP/M Glen Ellyn, Chicago, IL. . . . . (312) 469-2597*
RCP/M Granada Hills, CA . . . . (213) 360-5053*
RCP/M Ham Radio, Morton Grove, IL. . . . . (312) 967-0052
RCP/M Logan Square, Chicago, IL. . . . . (312) 252-2136*
RCP/M Los Angeles, CA. . . . . (213) 296-5927*
RCP/M MCBBS Keith Petersen, Royal Oak, MI . . . . (313) 759-6569 rb.
RCP/M Mid-Suffolk, Long Island, NY. . . . . (516) 751-5639—
RCP/M Mission, KA . . . . &(913) 362-9583*
RCP/M Mississauga HUG, Toronto, Ont., CN. . . . . $&(416) 232-2644*
RCP/M NEI, Chicago, IL. . . . . &(312) 949-6189—
RCP/M North Chicago, Chicago, IL. . . . . (312) 937-5639
RCP/M Olympia, WA . . . . (206) 357-7400*
RCP/M Oxgate, College Station, TX. . . . . !(409) 845-0509*
RCP/M Oxgate 001, Saratoga, CA . . . . $&(408) 354-5934*
RCP/M Oxgate 007, Grafton, VA. . . . . (804) 898-7493*
RCP/M Programmers Anonymous, Gorham, ME . . . . &(207) 839-2337*
RCP/M Providence, Providence, RI. . . . . (401) 751-5025 rb.
RCP/M RBBS AIMS, Hinsdale, IL. . . . . (312) 789-0499*
RCP/M RBBS Allentown, PA . . . . (215) 398-3937*
RCP/M RBBS AlphaNet, Lawrence, KA . . . . (913) 843-4259—
RCP/M RBBS Arvada Elect., Colorado Springs, CO . . . . (303) 598-4662*
RCP/M RBBS Bethesda, MD. . . . . (301) 229-3196
RCP/M RBBS BHEC, Baltimore, MD. (301) 661-2175*
RCP/M RBBS Cincinnati, OH. . . . . (513) 489-0149—
RCP/M RBBS Comp. Tech. Assoc., El Paso, TX. . . . . (915) 533-2202*
RCP/M RBBS Computron, Edmonton, Alberta, CN . . . . (403) 482-6854*
RCP/M RBBS Cranford, NJ. . . . . (201) 272-1874*
RCP/M RBBS DataTech 001, San Carlos, CA . . . . #1$&(415) 595-0541*
RCP/M RBBS DataTech 007, San Jose, CA. . . . . !(408) 238-9621*
RCP/M RBBS DataTech 010, Sunnyvale, CA . . . . !(408) 732-9190+
RCP/M RBBS El Paso, TX. . . . . &!(915) 598-1668*
RCP/M RBBS Fort Mill, SC. . . . . (803) 548-0900*
RCP/M RBBS GFRN Data Exch., Palos Verdes, CA . . . . $&(213) 541-2503*
RCP/M RBBS Hawkeye-PC, Cedar Rapids, IA . . . . (319) 363-3314

RCP/M RBBS Helena Valley, Helena, MT. . . . . (406) 443-2768+
RCP/M RBBS Hollywood, CA . . . . (213) 653-6398*
RCP/M RBBS IBM-PC, Hawthorne, CA . . . . $!(213) 973-2374
RCP/M RBBS IBM-PC, Orlando, FL . . . . $&!(305) 830-4340*
RCP/M RBBS JUG, Jacksonville, FL. . . . . $!(904) 725-4995*
RCP/M RBBS Lakewood, Denver, CO . . . . (303) 985-1108*
RCP/M RBBS Laurel, MD. . . . . (301) 953-3753*
RCP/M RBBS Larkspur, CA . . . . (415) 461-7726*
RCP/M RBBS Marin County, CA. . . . . (415) 383-0473*
RCP/M RBBS NACS/UAH, Huntsville, AL . . . . (205) 895-6749*rb.
RCP/M RBBS Napa Valley, CA. . . . . (707) 257-6502*
RCP/M RBBS Ocean, NJ . . . . &(201) 775-8705
RCP/M RBBS Orlando, FL . . . . $&!(305) 671-2330*
RCP/M RBBS Pasadena, CA. . . . . $(213) 577-9947*
RCP/M RBBS Paul Bogdanovich, NJ . . . . (201) 747-7301
RCP/M RBBS Pegasus, Houston, TX. . . . . !(713) 862-1624*
RCP/M RBBS Pickerington, OH. . . . . (614) 837-3269
RCP/M RBBS Piconet, Mt. View, CA. . . . . !(415) 965-4097
RCP/M RBBS Pinecliffe, CO . . . . &(303) 598-3995*
RCP/M RBBS Rutgers, New Brunswick, NJ. . . . . (201) 932-3879*
RCP/M RBBS San Diego, CA. . . . . $&(619) 273-4354*
RCP/M RBBS San Jose Oxgate, San Jose, CA. . . . . (408) 287-5901*
RCP/M RBBS SDCS San Diego, CA. !(619) 236-0742*
RCP/M RBBS SDCS HEC#04, La Mesa, CA. . . . . !(619) 461-0111—
RCP/M RBBS Southfield, MI . . . . (313) 559-5326*
RCP/M RBBS Tampa, FL. . . . . $(813) 831-7276
RCP/M RBBS Woodstock, NY. . . . . &(914) 679-8734*
RCP/M RBBS Yelm, Olympia, WA. (206) 458-3086 rb.
RCP/M Rich & Famous, San Francisco, CA . . . . (415) 552-9968*
RCP/M Satsuma, Houston, TX. . . . . &!(713) 469-8893—
RCP/M Simi Valley, CA . . . . (805) 527-2219—
RCP/M SJBBS Bearsville, NY. . . . . (914) 679-6559*rb.
RCP/M SJBBS Johnson City, NY . . . . (607) 797-6416—
RCP/M Software Tools, Sydney, Australia 61 02 997-1018*
RCP/M Sunnyvale, CA . . . . (408) 730-8733—
RCP/M Superbrain, Lexington, MA . . . . $&(617) 862-0781*
RCP/M System One, Toronto, Ontario, CN. . . . . &(416) 231-9538*
RCP/M System Two, Toronto, Ontario, CN . . . . &(416) 231-1262*
RCP/M Technical, Houston, TX. . . . . !(713) 522-3805 rb.
RCP/M Technical, Thousand Oaks, CA . . . . &(805) 492-5472*
RCP/M The C-Line, NJ. . . . . (201) 625-1797—
RCP/M W. Carrolton, Dayton, OH. (513) 435-5201*

Remote Northstar Denver, CO. . . . . (303) 444-7231
Remote Northstar NASA, Greenbelt, MD. . . . . (301) 344-9156
Remote Northstar Santa Barbara, CA . . . . (805) 964-4115
Remote Northstar Virginia Beach, VA . . . . (804) 340-5246

ST80-CC Lance Micklus, Inc., Burlington, VT . . . . #1(802) 862-7023*
ST80-PBB Monroe Camera Shop, Monroe, NY . . . . (914) 782-7605

TBBS Akron, OH . . . . (216) 724-2125*
TBBS Akron, OH . . . . (216) 724-1963*
TBBS Aurora, CO . . . . #1!(303) 690-4566
TBBS Austin, TX . . . . #1!(512) 385-1102*
TBBS Beer City, Milwaukee, WI . . . . &(414) 355-8839*
TBBS Canopus, Milwaukee, WI . . . . (414) 281-0545*
TBBS Exidy 2000, Houston, TX . . . . &(713) 442-7644*
TBBS Freelancin' Alvin, Houston, TX . . . . &(713) 331-2599*
TBBS Freelancin', Houston, TX . . . . &(713) 488-2003*
TBBS Hawkins, TX . . . . &(214) 769-3036*
TBBS Noah's Ark, Fremont, CA . . . . !(415) 490-8083*so.
TBBS Pizza-Net, Orlando, FL . . . . !(305) 645-5543*
TBBS Shreveport, LA . . . . !(318) 635-8660*
TBBS Tulsa, OK . . . . !(918) 749-0059*

TCBBS Astrocom, New York, NY . . . . #1(212) 799-4649*
TCBBS B.A.M.S. New York, NY . . . . (212) 362-1040*

T-NET Central Processing Unit . . . . (313) 453-5146*
T-NET Delta Connection . . . . (609) 896-2436*
T-NET Special Corp . . . . (313) 855-6321*
T-NET Twilight Phone, Warren, MI . . . . #1(313) 775-1649*

TRADE-80 Albany, GA . . . . (912) 439-7740*
TRADE-80 Fort Lauderdale, FL . . . . #1(305) 525-1192
TRADE-80 Omaha, NE . . . . (402) 292-6184

Miscellaneous or Unknown System Types

(?) Queens, NY . . . . (718) 896-0519
Access-80, Tampa, FL . . . . (813) 884-1506*
Adventure BBS, Roslyn, NY . . . . (516) 621-9296
Adventurer's Tavern, San Diego, CA . . . . (619) 583-3103
Alpha, Tampa, FL (account no.=ABCD00, password=
TRYIT) . . . . (813) 969-0512*
Aphrodite-E, Patterson, NJ . . . . (201) 831-1042 so.
Apollo's Chariot, Apollo, FL . . . . (813) 645-3669
Applecrackers, Columbus, OH . . . . (614) 475-9791*
Apple Crunch, Houston, TX . . . . (713) 468-3122
ARBB Seattle, WA . . . . (206) 546-6239
Atatcom/80 San Leandro, CA . . . . !(415) 895-8980*
Atari BBS, Virginia Beach, VA . . . . (804) 491-1437*

Austin Party Board, Austin, TX. . . . . (512) 442-1116*
Aviators Bulletin Board, Sacramento, CA . . . . (916) 393-4459
BBS Apollo, Phoenix, AZ . . . . (602) 246-1432*
BBS Atari AMIS, Kansas City, MO . . . . !(816) 587-9543*
BBS Commodore, San Juan, Puerto Rico . . . . (809) 781-0350—
BBS Computer Applications Co., Poland, OH . . . . (216) 757-3711
BBS-80 DALTRUG, Dallas, TX . . . . !(214) 289-1386*
BBS Heathkit Store, Warwick, RI . . . . !(401) 738-5152—
BBS Homestead, FL. . . . . (305) 246-1111
BBS MCUA, Houston, TX . . . . (713) 661-5428*
BBS Pensacola, FL. . . . . (904) 477-8783
BBS-16 Santa Rosa, CA . . . . !(707) 527-5908
BBS SUE Milwaukee, WI . . . . (414) 327-6010
BBS Syslink, Providence, RI . . . . !(401) 272-1138*
BBS The BULL, Toronto, Ontario, CN. . . . . (416) 423-3265 so.
BBS The Safehouse, Minneapolis, MN . . . . !(612) 724-7066*
Big Top Games System, Milwaukee, WI . . . . (414) 259-9475
Bird House, San Jose, CA. . . . . (408) 267-7399
BJ/Rustex, Worcester, MA . . . . !(617) 757-8499—
Blax-80 BBS, Phoenix, AZ . . . . (602) 952-1382*
Boston Information Exchange, Boston, MA. . . . . &(617) 423-6985*
Bradley Computer BBS, Tampa, FL. . . . . (813) 734-7103
BSBB Tampa, FL . . . . (813) 885-6187
Call-A-Lawyer, Phoenix, AZ . . . . (602) 275-6644*
Capital City BBS, Albany, NY. . . . . (518) 346-3596*
Cass-80 Hickory Hills, IL. . . . . (312) 598-4861
C-HUG Bulletin Board, Fairfax, VA . . . . (703) 360-3812*
C.M.M.S. Chicago, IL . . . . (312) 957-3924*
Cohoes Forum, Cohoes, NY . . . . (518) 235-9073
COLOUR-80, Orange Park, FL . . . . !(904) 264-0335*
Commodore Video King, Skokie, IL . . . . (312) 674-6502
Compuque-80, Houston, TX . . . . &(713) 444-7041*
Compusystems, Columbia, SC. . . . . (803) 771-0922
Computer Connection, Beverly Hills, CA. . . . . (213) 657-1799
Computers for Christ, Ontario, CA . . . . (714) 983-9923*
Creepy Corridors, Phoenix, AZ . . . . !(602) 956-5021—
CVBBS, San Diego, CA . . . . (619) 691-8367*
Datamate, Canoga Park, CA . . . . #1(213) 998-7992 so.
Diamond III, Phoenix, AZ. . . . . (602) 890-0972*
Dimension-80 Orange, CA. . . . . (714) 974-9788
Download-80 Mojo's, Forest Knolls, CA. . . . . &(415) 488-9145*
Dragon's Game System, Long Beach, CA. . . . . (213) 428-5206
Drummer, San Francisco, CA . . . . (415) 552-7671 so.
EMC-80 St. Louis, MO. . . . . (314) 645-1047
Experimental-80 Kansas City, MO . . . . (913) 676-3613
FBBS #1, Purdue, IN. . . . . &$(317) 494-6643*
Future Tech, Alexandria, VA . . . . (703) 451-4893*

GABBS, Armadillo Media, Houston, TX....................!(713) 444-7098*
GABBS, Food for Thought, Omaha, NB ....!(402) 551-4618
GABBS, Houston, TX...............................#1!(713) 455-9502*
GABBS, Mindstorm, Terre Haute, IN ....!(812) 235-0908*
GABBS, Vox Populi, Houston, TX.......................!(713) 772-6096*
GBBSII Apple PI Bloomfield, CO.........................!(303) 469-7541*
GBBSII Aurora-Net, Denver, CO ....!(303) 343-8401*
GBBSII Denver, CO ....!(303) 693-1064—
GBBSII Eamon, Denver, CO ....$!(303) 750-3783—
GBBSII Off The Wall, Denver, CO ....!(303) 443-3367*
Genesys, Phoenix, AZ...............................(602) 967-4529*
Grape Line BBS, Napa Valley, CA......................!(707) 538-9124*
Hermes-80 Allentown, PA.............................(215) 434-3998
HEX Silver Spring, MD................................%(301) 593-7033*
IBM PC No-Name, San Lorenzo, CA.................&!(415) 481-0252*
INFOEX-80 Tulsa, OK................................!(918) 838-8698*
INFOEX-80 West Palm Beach, FL.......................(305) 683-6044*
Interface BBS (Atari), Chicago, IL.........................(312) 296-3883
Irvine Line, Irvine, CA....................................(714) 551-4336
JCTS Redmond, WA...................................(206) 883-0403*
L.A. Interchange, Los Angeles, CA........................(213) 631-3186*
Lethbridge Gaming System, Lethbridge, AB, CN ....(403) 320-6923
Living BBS, Education SIG ....!(415) 565-3037
Mages Inn, Omaha, NE ....(402) 734-4748*
Magus, Herndon, VA ....(703) 471-0611*
Mail Board-82, Seattle, WA ....(206) 527-0897*
Micro-Com, Cincinnati, OH ....!(513) 671-2753
Micro-Com, Louisville, OH...............................(216) 875-4582*
Micro-80 West Palm Beach, FL.............................(305) 686-3695
Micro Informer, Tampa, FL...............................(813) 875-3331
Microsystems, Phoenix, AZ ....(602) 938-4508*
Midwest, St. Louis, MO ....(314) 227-4312 so.
Mini-Bin, Seattle, WA ....(206) 762-5141*
MMMMel Rey, CA......................................!(213) 452-6111
MMMMMM#1, Santa Monica, CA.......................!(213) 390-3239
MMMMMM#2, New York, NY ....!(212) 541-5975
MMMMMM#4, Lawndale, CA ....!(213) 821-2257
Motherboard, San Leandro, CA..........................!(415) 352-8442
MPC The DUNGEON, New Orleans, LA ....!(504) 245-8920*
NBBS Norfolk, VA ....(804) 444-3392
Nibble One, Schenectady, NY...........................(518) 370-8343
North Orange County Computer Club, Orange, CA ....(714) 633-5240
Novation CO., Los Angeles, CA (password=CAT).............(213) 881-6880
NWLAIBMPCUG, Shreveport, LA........................!(318) 688-7078
NWWCUG Edmunds, Seattle, WA ....(206) 743-6021
Nybbles-80 Elmsford, NY ....(718) 626-0375
OACPM Omaha, NE ....(402) 292-9598*

OARCS Portland, OR . . . . (503) 641-2798
OCTUG Orange County, Garden Grove, CA . . . . (714) 530-8226
Omega, Phoenix, AZ . . . . (602) 952-2018*
Oracle North Hollywood, CA . . . . (213) 980-5643 so.
Orange County Data Exchange, Garden Grove, CA . . . . (714) 537-7913
OS-9 6809 BBS, Palatine, IL . . . . (312) 397-8308
PBBS Arc-Net, Little Rock, AR . . . . !(501) 372-0576*
PBBS Co-operative Comp. Svc., Palatine, IL . . . . (312) 359-9450*
Personal Msg. System-80, Deerfield Bch, FL . . . . &(305) 427-6300*
PHOTO-80, Haledon, NJ . . . . (201) 790-6795
PMBBS . . . . (713) 441-4032
Potomac Micro Magic Inc., Falls Church, VA . . . . (703) 379-0303*
RACS V Fullerton, CA . . . . (714) 524-1228
RBBS Milwaukee-Chicago Line . . . . (312) 876-0974
RIBBS Houston, TX . . . . (713) 497-5433
R.I.C.A.M.I.S., Kingston, RI . . . . !(401) 456-8250*
RI Tandy Users Group, Cranston, RI . . . . !(401) 944-4689*
RS-CPM Clarksville, MI . . . . (616) 693-2648
SATUG BBS, San Antonio, TX . . . . (512) 494-0285
Seacomm-80 Seattle, WA . . . . (206) 763-8879*
SIGNON Reno, NV (password=FREE) . . . . (702) 826-7234
. . . . $(702) 826-7277
SISTER Staten Island, NY . . . . (718) 442-3874*
SOBBS Poor Man's BBS, Houston, TX . . . . (713) 453-7931*
Stellar III, Phoenix, AZ . . . . (602) 833-0740*
Steve's BBS, Shawnee Mission, KS . . . . (913) 648-5301*
Stuart II, Boulder Creek, CA . . . . !#1(408) 338-9511*
Sunrise Omega-80, Oakland, CA . . . . (415) 452-0350
Switchboard, Alexandria, VA . . . . (703) 765-2161*
System/80 San Leandro, CA . . . . (415) 782-4402
Talk-80 ROBB, Portsmouth, VA . . . . (804) 484-9636
TCUG BBS, Washington, DC . . . . (703) 836-0384*
Tech-Link, Forest Glen, MD . . . . (301) 565-9051*
TECOM-80, Tampa, FL . . . . (813) 839-6746
Telcom 7 New Fairfield, CT . . . . (203) 746-5763*
Telemessage-80, Atlanta, GA . . . . (404) 962-0616
The Garden of Eden, Phoenix, AZ . . . . !(602) 991-0144*
The Interface, Los Angeles, CA . . . . (213) 477-4605
Toledo Apple Users BBS, Toledo, OH . . . . (419) 537-9777*
Treasure Island, Royal Oak, MI . . . . (313) 547-7903
Vanmil, Milwaukee, WI . . . . (414) 271-7580*
VERGA 80, Santa Ana, CA . . . . (714) 547-6220
Vic-20 Online, Houston, TX . . . . (713) 944-6597*
Visiboard, Wellesley, MA . . . . (617) 235-5082
Voyager, Phoenix, AZ . . . . (602) 247-6034
WAPABBS, Charlotte, NC . . . . (704) 373-7966*
Westside Download, Detroit, MI . . . . (313) 348-4479

GLOSSARY

Our Personal Dictionary of Jargon

Access: Connecting a terminal or computer to another computer or storage device. Often used as a transitive verb, as in "I have accessed The Source computer and data base."

Acoustic coupler: A type of modem that connects a computer system to a telephone line by inserting a standard telephone handset into two cups that are attached directly to the modem.

Address: Used as a noun, it refers to an exact storage location of memory data in a chip or other storage device. Used as a verb, it refers to the act of storing data in a specific location in memory.

Algorithm: A predetermined set of instructions for solving a specific problem in a finite number of steps.

Alphanumeric: Refers to data that consist of numbers and letters.

ALU: An abbreviation for Arithmetic Logic Unit, the portion of the computer that performs arithmetic and logical operations.

Answerback: Used in Western Union and Telex communications, it is a code by which the receiving device identifies the sending device.

Append: Adding additional data to the end of an existing file.

ASCII: American Standard Code for Information Interchange. The code, used on most desk-top computers, was established to achieve compatibility between various types of equipment. It assigns a one-byte code to every English alphabet letter, number, special character and control character.

Asynchronous: A method of data transmission where the sender and receiver don't have to be synchronized, bit for bit. It is the most common method of data communication for small computers and one of three different methods of coordinating the sending and receiving of data. Both sender and receiver must use the same method.

Auto answer: A feature in some modems that allows them to answer an incoming call and process it.

Auto dial: A feature in many modems that allows the user to initiate a phone call by inserting commands from the keyboard or other devices.

Automatic message switching: A technique that automatically routes incoming messages to an appropriate designation by means of information contained in the message itself.

Backup: To duplicate hardware, software or data.

Backup copy: A duplicate of the original version of data or software that is made in case the original is destroyed.

BASIC: An acronym for Beginner's All-Purpose Symbolic Instruction Code, a programming language widely taught as the first such language in schools. It is the principal language in many minicomputers and microcomputers.

Baud: A unit of measurement that describes the number of bits transmitted per second. A system that transmits 300 bits per second is transmitting at 300 Baud.

Bell System 103: The standard frequency used by 300-Baud modems. Other systems are the Bell 113, which is an originate-only system and should be avoided. The standard system for a 1,200-Baud modem is the Bell 212A, so if you buy a 1200-Baud modem, ensure that it is compatible with Bell 212A.

Binary: Refers to a code in which the digits 1 and 0 are used to describe numbers. It also refers to a condition where there are only two possible choices, such as on/off; true/false; yes/no.

Bisynchronous: Along with Asynchronous and Synchronous, this is one of three methods of coordinating the sending and receiving of data. Both sender and receiver systems must use the same method.

Bit: Contraction of binary digit, the smallest unit of storage in a computer system; a 1 or 0 at a particular location within a CPU or memory.

Boolean algebra: An algebra that expresses logical concepts in mathematical form and uses such logical operations as AND, OR, NOR and IF–THEN. It is the logical basis for modern computers.

Boot: To activate a computer or program. Usually this means simply to turn the thing on.

Bubble memory: A solid-state memory device that stores large amounts of data in a small space and has fast access time. The memory is retained even when the computer is shut down.

Buffer: A storage area used to temporarily hold data being transferred from one device to another.

Bundled: A term describing the packaging of software, services and hardware for sale at a single price.

Bus: A circuit for the transfer of electronic signals between two devices.

Byte: A group of consecutive bits tied together to represent a single character or number. In modern computers, a byte usually consists of eight bits.

Card: A printed circuit board inserted into a computer to provide additional memory or functions.

Chip: Electronic circuits etched onto a tiny disc, generally of silicon. Chips perform the same functions as wired-together transistors, resistors and such.

Color monitors: Color displays for desk-top computers are generated by two different methods. One of these is "composite color," a 40-column display limited to eight colors and, while suitable for games, usually lacking the definition needed for word processing and other more serious needs. (See Composite video listing.) The second system is "RGB color," which can display 80 and more columns across the screen and, in some configurations, a nearly infinite number of colors. In general, RGB color has better definition and is more expensive. (See RGB monitors and RGB video.)

Composite video: A one-wire signal that combines both the horizontal and vertical sync pulses, used to prevent vertical and horizontal roll. When color is added to a composite video signal, it is called a composite color signal.

CP-M: See Operating system.

CPU: Central processing unit; a chip that performs addition, division, sorting or other logical operations required to run computer programs. An 8-bit CPU can process eight pieces of information at one time, a 16-bit CPU, 16 pieces, etc. In general, microcomputers use 8-bit or 16-bit CPUs, minicomputers 16- or 32-bit, and mainframes can use several different CPUs.

CRT is the abbreviation for cathode ray tube, a screen like that of a television receiver, used in computer systems for viewing data. It typically displays 20 to 24 lines of data with 40 to 80 characters per line.

Daisy wheel printer: An impact printer that prints fully formed characters with one strike, like a typewriter. Its typefaces radiate out from a wheellike disc.

Data base: An electronic collection of similar records, such as a data base of magazine titles.

DCE/DTE: Data Communications Equipment/Data Terminal Equipment. All devices connecting to an RS-232 interface must either be a DCE (such as a modem or printer) or a DTE (computer or terminal). This defines which device will talk and which will listen.

Default: A built-in value assigned to a software program but which is changeable by the user.

Disk or Disc: A magnetic disk, or platter, resembling a phonograph record, which provides electronic storage for data.

Disk drive: A unit that reads and writes data stored on a disk. The drive rotates the disk and reads the information, somewhat like a small phonograph player reading a record.

Dot matrix: A printed character formed by dots laid closely together that gives the impression of having been printed by a fully formed type face. The dots are formed by wire ends, jets of ink, electrical charges or laser beams.

Download: The receiving of an entire data file, or program, from another computer system. Sending the file or program to another system is called uploading.

Dumb terminal: The minimum equipment necessary to communicate with a computer. It consists of a monitor and a keyboard and will do little more than send and receive data.

Dump: To transfer the entire contents of a file or RAM to a storage medium or to a printer.

Duplex: Full duplex is a method of data transmission that allows both modems to send and receive at the same time, like a phone conversation. Half duplex is one-way sending and receiving, like CB radio. Coordinated systems should use the same duplex mode.

Electronic mail: A technique that allows a computer user to send a message to another user's "mailbox" or to receive messages from the user's own mailbox.

EPROM: Acronym for erasable programmable read-only memory. A type of ROM chip that can be erased and reprogrammed by the user.

Firmware: Printed circuits that plug into a computer to make it perform extra functions. Some firmware duplicates functions performed by software.

Floppy disk: A thin magnetic disk (in a protective paper or plastic jacket) that stores data or programs. It's erasable and reusable and comes in several sizes. The standards, however, are 3½ inches, 5¼ inches and 8 inches.

Hacker: A computer obsessive.

Handshaking: The portion of a communications session in which the sender and receiver establish each other's identity and match up the necessary "protocols."

Hard copy: Computer output that is printed on paper. Soft copy is computer output that appears on the display screen.

Hard disk: A device to store data on magnetic disks that, unlike floppies, are rigid and not readily interchangeable; each one hold several million bytes and stores or retrieves data faster than a floppy.

Hardware: The physical parts of a computer: keyboard, viewing screen, disk drives, printer, chips, etc.

Host computer: A computer to which a number of terminals and/or other smaller computers are connected.

Interface: An electronic device that allows one component of a computer system to communicate with another. For example, an interface board is needed to connect the computer with the printer.

K: Abbreviation for kilo, usually referring to a thousand bytes of storage.

Language: Computer languages vary in their complexity, beginning with machine language, which is the native idiom of the CPU, the ones and zeroes of binary code. Next comes assembly language, which translates machine language into words and numbers more easily used by people. Above these are "high-level" languages such as BASIC (Beginner's All-Purpose Symbolic Instruction Code), COBOL (Common Business-Oriented Language) and FORTRAN (Formula Translation System).

Load: To transfer a program into main memory from an auxiliary storage device.

Local area networking: LAN, as the name implies, allows computerized equipment, including personal computer systems, to transfer information quickly and economically within a limited area, typically on the premises of a single enterprise or between a company's office and factory facilities. A local area network consists of the devices it links, the wire or cable used to carry data among them, and special circuitry (often on a board that plugs into these devices) that allows each terminal on the line to transmit and receive information common to the network.

Log on: The procedure of establishing contact with another system.

M: Abbreviation for megabyte, one million bytes.

Macro: Abbreviation for macroinstruction, a single instruction that represents a given sequence of instructions.

Mainframe: A large multi-user computer that utilizes several CPUs and many megabytes of storage.

Memory: Used to describe the internal working space of computers, their RAM and ROM capacity.

Microcomputer: A single-user ("personal") computer, usually with an 8- or 16-bit CPU.

Minicomputer: A computer with 16-bit or 32-bit CPU that can accommodate several users at once.

Modem: A piece of hardware, costing from $30 to beyond $1,000, that converts computer blips into telephone beeps at the sending end and reverses the process at the receiving end. The term is a combination of modulator/demodulator.

MS-DOS: For the disk operating system manufactured by Microsoft Corporation. See Operating system.

Nibble: Half of a byte, a unit of no special importance except to a hacker, particularly a hacker who is "de-protecting" a software program.

NTSC: An abbreviation for National Television Standards Committee. NTSC has set a broadcast standard for sync frequencies and video levels in composite video signals. Additionally, it standardizes the color-burst encoding in composite broadcast signals. Broadcasters must adhere to this standard when they transmit a composite video signal on the air.

Operating system: The program that acts as the foreman of the computer, coordinating the system including the CPU, disk drives, printer, modem and other programs. It is often called a disk operating system (DOS) because it controls the flow of data between the CPU and the disk drives. CP-M, APPLE DOS, MS-DOS and PC-DOS are the names of commonly used operating systems.

Packet switching: A technique in which data are sent from a sending to a receiving terminal or computer in packets of fixed length.

Parity, odd and even: A spot check for transmission errors. The sending computer adds a 1 or a 0 to the codes for each character to make the digits total an odd number (in odd parity) or an even number (even parity). The receiving machine totals the codes to make sure the sum is correctly even or odd. If incorrect, it flashes "error."

Peripherals: Hardware that is added to a computer to make up a system, such as a printer, disk drive, modem, etc.

Ports: The channels through which computers send and receive data. They are either serial or parallel. See Interface, which is synonymous with port.

RAM: Random access memory, a chip (or network of chips) that remembers (1) a program or file loaded into your computer from a disk, and (2) words or numbers you type in. RAM stores and retrieves data for your CPU much faster than disks, but erases if the power goes off—even for a split second.

RGB monitors: Conceptually simpler than composite monitors, they produce a superior display. They are also quite a bit more expensive than the average composite monitor. RGB monitors come in several price ranges, and their prices are directly related to the resolution of the display. Medium resolution RGB monitors typically display 370 horizontal points and 235 vertical points. High resolution RGB monitors can display about twice this resolution, or 720×512 points. The most important factor in determining the resolution of a display is the spot size of the red, green and blue phosphor on the CRT screen itself. Spot size for a medium-resolution display is 0.6 mm or less, with high-resolution spot size being 0.3 mm.

There are also two distinct types of RGB monitors: analog and digital. With an analog RGB monitor you can vary the intensity of each gun from zero to full brightness, allowing an infinite set of colors to be displayed. In contrast, a digital RGB monitor can turn a gun on or off, but is incapable of varying the intensity in between. Thus a digital RGB monitor is limited to displaying only (2×2×2=) 8 distinct colors. Analog RGB monitors are the most flexible and can display either a digital or analog signal. Digital RGB monitors cannot display an analog RGB signal.

RGB video makes use of several wires and signals to independently control each color gun. RGB video is much more clear and sharp than composite color video for a couple of reasons. First, the signal does not have to be encoded into a composite signal at the computer and decoded at the monitor. This allows more precise displays with the computer directly controlling the color guns in the monitor. Second, each gun can be switched on and off extremely rapidly, eliminating any blur that may occur from one color to the next.

ROM: Read only memory; a chip that can be read but cannot be written over or otherwise altered. ROM provides permanent instructions prewritten by the manufacturer to get the computer started when the power is first turned on, to store the shapes of characters needed for the display and to store certain program commands.

Smart terminal: A computer terminal that can do more than the dumb terminal, and is therefore smarter. Its ability to store information is a key characteristic.

Software: The instructions by which a computer operates. Also known as programs, software comes on floppy disks for small computers and on magnetic tape for larger ones.

Tape drives: Some less expensive computers use tape recorders instead of disk drives to store information and programs. Tape drives tend to be much slower than disk drives, although large improvements are being made.

Terminal: A device used to send and receive data from a computer system, especially such a device with a keyboard and video display.

Winchester disk: See hard disk.

Zero bit: The leftmost high-order bit in a word or byte.

INDEX

About the Author

DAVID CHANDLER is a writer and journalist of more than twenty years' experience and the author of three history books. His investigative reporting has won several national awards, including a Pulitzer Prize. A former correspondent for *Life* magazine and the Associated Press, he lives in Florida and Colorado, and he writes for *People* magazine.